Nazis and Nudists

A Baby Boomer's Memoir of Love and Journalism from
Psychedelic Mushrooms to Pig-on-a-Spit

David Haldane

© 2015 by David Haldane

All rights reserved. No part of this book may be reproduced, stored in a retrieval system or transmitted in any form or by any means without the prior written permission of the publishers, except by a reviewer who may quote brief passages in a review to be printed in a newspaper, magazine or journal.

The final approval for this literary material is granted by the author.

First printing

The author has tried to recreate events, locales and conversations from memory. In order to maintain anonymity in some instances, the author may have changed the names of individuals and places. The author may have changed some identifying characteristics and details such as physical properties, occupations and places of residence.

ISBN: 978-1-61296-593-2
PUBLISHED BY BLACK ROSE WRITING
www.blackrosewriting.com

Printed in the United States of America
Suggested retail price $15.95

Nazis and Nudists is printed in Times New Roman

To my wife, Ivy, who came from a small island to make my life large.

Contents

Author's Note	6
Prologue: Boats with Holes	8
A Death in the Magic Kingdom	15
Toking in a Trailer	18
Manson's Lawyer	22
Worms	28
Politico	33
Baseball Bats	38
Whispers in a Graveyard	45
Each According to His Need	48
Chillin with a Chillum	55
Nazis	60
Nudists	65
Getting Off	69
Jerusalem	75
What the Voices Say	83
Little Boxes	91

Sodom and Gomorrah	95
Mummies	101
A Ghost on the Tracks	107
Druggies with Knives	111
Wading into the Mainstream	117
Seizing the Times	122
Small Dark Rooms	125
Looking Toward the Light	130
Losing Leary	136
Stalking the Golden Calf	144
Head on a Stick	149
Filipina Heart	153
Karma	157
Pig-on-a-Spit	161
Heart in the Ceiling	165
My Imported Bride	171
The End Times	177
Green Leafy Space	183
Epilogue: Holding Down the Fort	187
Acknowledgements	190

ii.

Author's Note

This is a work of nonfiction. As a series of autobiographical essays loosely comprising a memoir, it is highly subjective and prone to the vagaries of time and memory. But it is also the work of a journalist who, over many years of practicing that craft, has fancied himself possessed of a mind and pen honed into objective instruments of observation. Perhaps you can appreciate the challenge: how to integrate those two very distinct – and sometimes conflicting – voices.

I don't claim to have accomplished that here. What I do hope, however, is to have provided an entertaining and informative tour of a span of time important both in our history and in my life. It was an era pregnant with expectation and the intoxicating excitement of a new age to come. The fact that the new age never arrived in no way lessens the period's impact on those who experienced it or those who came after, though for many the intoxication led to a kind of madness.

For me, the late 1960s and early 1970s was a formative time, a time that made me what I am today and still looms large in my consciousness. This is the story, not only of those times, but of what came later, of a personal struggle – shared by many of my generation – to find extrication from faraway and strange environs of the heart to somewhere resembling home. It was a lifelong search that led through many alien pastures ending, in my case anyway, in an unexpected and exotic place of peace.

Wherever possible I have confirmed memory with other sources, sometimes including my own published and unpublished writings from the era in question. In some instances, I have telescoped events and revised sequences for dramatic effect. In most cases, I have used people's real names. When that proved impossible, due to the failings of memory or research, I have employed pseudonyms. To those in both categories, I beg forgiveness.

Finally, in borrowing from my own past works I have on occasion borrowed liberally. Thus portions of this book are based on material originally published in different form in the *Los Angeles Times, Los Angeles Times Magazine, Berkeley BARB, Islands, Orange Coast, Links, Aqua* and *Chicken Soup for the Single's Soul.* In the highly unlikely event that anyone experiences déjà vu, I apologize.

David Haldane
October, 2015

iii.

Prologue: Boats with Holes

We were a mile off the coast of a remote Philippine island when I realized that the boat was sinking. Perhaps, I mused, it was because of those holes. One was in the gas tank, which meant that we were stranded; the other in the hull, which meant that we'd be swamped. The plain truth was that we were taking on water like, well, a boat with two holes.

"Hey Loloy," I called out to the captain and our guide, "is this normal?"

"Mr. David," he implored with a toothy grin, "do not worry." Putting aside all pretense of dignity, I grabbed a red sweatshirt, waved it like a flag, and started to yell.

A more seaworthy vessel had brought my wife, Ivy, and I here in the first place to Surigao City, Mindanao, where East meets West in the historic homeland of the Muslim Moros better known for be-headings than for badminton. But we'd come looking for a place to *live*, not to die. And to live you need a house, so it was that for which we'd come looking. We'd seen lots of them too; everything from a shabby shack overlooking a broken brick wall to a three-story mansion with a view.

For quite a while, in fact, that had been our favorite. Until we noticed the gaping crack in its lower wall; evidence, we were told, that this *mansion* was built on the foundation for a *house*. "I'm not saying it will collapse," our structural engineer said, "but I can't promise you it won't."

Then we heard of Punta Bilar. Ivy, who was born in the Philippines and speaks the local language, taught me how to say it. "Pooonta Beelar," she said, emphasizing the ooos and the eees. "It means Point Watch."

"Let's go see it," I suggested, and so we did.

What I discovered was that the place is aptly named. Within

Surigao City limits though several miles outside of town, it is a verdant finger of land pointing elegantly north toward the distant island of Leyte. It was at the very tip of this finger, on a windy tropical morning, that we came to the site we loved: a thousand square meters of untended farmland lilting lazily down towards the shore. At its base meandered a solitary highway, following the contours of the coast like a tight pair of jeans. And tucked neatly into one of its lower corners, as if in an Edward Hopper painting, a lovely white lighthouse peered longingly out to sea.

Our excitement rising, Ivy and I scrambled up the hill to catch the view. It was breathtaking. Off in the distance, under billowing clouds, we could see islands whose names we did not know. "This will be the view from our porch," she whispered, giving my hand a gentle squeeze. I squeezed hers back.

"I think this is it," I said, "I think that we're home." The only question now was how to make it happen. Then we got stuck in the boat with two holes.

Despite our boatman's assurances, the situation looked grim. We had enlisted him and his wife – one of Ivy's cousins – to ferry us to Bucas Grande, one of the Philippines' most beautiful islands. The mode of transportation was their 25-foot pamboat, a narrow motorized vessel with pontoons. About thirty minutes into what should have been a three-hour trip, however, a sickening crunch brought everything to a screeching halt. Navigating too close to shore in shallow water, we'd hit a rock and broken the propeller.

"No worries," Loloy insisted, pointing a bony finger toward the shore, "I will fix while you rest on the beach."

So my wife and I helped pull the injured craft ashore and spent the next several hours under a coconut tree drinking rum. When the repairs were completed, we all clamored back aboard and got underway. But two hours later the engine sputtered and stopped again; this time, Loloy explained after a thorough inspection, because a previously unnoticed leak in the gas tank had relieved us of our fuel.

I didn't *really* get nervous, though, until I saw Ivy and her cousin bailing water from the bow. "Oh yes," the boatman added, "and there's another crack in the hull." Apparently, I surmised, our earlier collision with the bottom had left an unrepaired fissure under the water line that, though invisible to us, was a veritable gateway to the ocean.

Feeling the rising fangs of panic gnawing at the edges of my stomach, I checked for a cell signal and found none. My question about life jackets drew only blank stares. There were, however, several wooden paddles aboard and so for a while we bailed and paddled in shifts, aiming for the horizon on which we could barely discern the outlines of that distant island. An hour later they hadn't moved any closer. And that's when the gentle nibbles of panic became like the bites of a bear, prompting me to grab that red sweatshirt and loudly start to swear.

My life passed before me like a slow rumbling train, and I thought of another train, the one that circles Disneyland. How many summer afternoons I'd spent watching it as a child. Where had all those afternoons gone, and by whose authority? All the miles and decades I'd traveled, from the innocent safety of indifference to the crumbling shoals of pseudo revolution; from deep valleys of drug-induced stupor to soaring mountaintops beneath the nose of God, and all for what? To, like Moses' dumb cousin, perish within sight of the Promised Land? I didn't think so. Though my companions had not joined in my antics, they definitely looked concerned.

"Honey *calm down*," Ivy said, looking distinctly embarrassed.

"Sir David," Loloy implored, twisting a strand of his silky black hair. "*Please* – we are OK."

It turned out that he was right; twenty minutes later – and having nothing to do with my frantic theatrics – a passing octopus fisherman offered a tow. There are moments in life when certain insights are unavoidable. As we eased our way slowly toward harbor with the air tasting especially sweet and our nostrils flaring with the smell of salt, I couldn't help but notice the demeanor of my fellow travelers. It was exactly the same now as it had been in the crisis: smiling, calm, steadfast and trusting. I had observed this cultural trait before; the simple unflappable Filipino faith that, no matter what happens and despite overwhelming evidence to the contrary, everything will be all right.

As I thought of it now, though, the quality seemed to take on an almost spiritual dimension as if it were a thing unto itself, a separate entity like gas or like air. Perhaps, I thought, it was a function more of place than of people; an ethereal substance that clung to the land and the sea. Whatever it was, it seemed to have a magnetic effect, a power that drew any imbiber into its holy embrace. And what it imparted was a special sense of *rootedness* that I had never felt before, a gift offering some relief from the uncertainties of time and space.

It was this indefinable quality, I now realized, that had brought me to these shores. And it was in its spirit that, tying up at the island's only village, Loloy promised to fix the boat quickly and continue our tour. Though I admired his pluck, I did not share it and so firmly declined. No worries, he said cheerfully, "I have a cousin in town."

What followed was a long night of torture. Lying on the hard floor of a sweltering house with mosquitoes in my ears and howling dogs outside, I listened for hours to the cousin's jarring snore. It rattled like a minor earthquake, then lapsed into long breathless silences during which I was certain he had died. Through it all I lay staring at the ceiling wondering whether it would be better to have been lost at sea.

Getting up early has never been my forte, but on this particular morning it was easy. After a breakfast of mangos and dried fish, Ivy and I thanked our host and made for the dock where we paid a modest fare to climb aboard a large commercial ferry with a working engine and, we hoped, not even *one* hole.

We were still standing on the dock when we caught a glimpse of Loloy and his wife. They had shoved off from the beach in their reconstituted pamboat, supposedly repaired the day before, and were waving enthusiastically as they headed out. Before they could lower their hands, however, the boat's motor coughed twice and quit. Loloy looked mildly confused as his wife paddled them back toward the shore. The last thing I saw was him standing with hands on his hips, kicking the bow but still full of smiles.

I thought of that enigmatic smile as we slid out from the harbor. I wanted to feel it, to absorb it, to make it my own. Mostly I wanted it to carry me home. Whether that was a physical place or a place of the heart, I didn't yet know. Perhaps it was both. What I did know was that I had spent much of my life trying to get there.

Nazis and Nudists

David Haldane

1.

A Death in the Magic Kingdom

I was 15 the day my classmate made history by standing in a bobsled. He didn't notice the low-hanging tunnel up ahead. So he unbuckled his seat belt to show off for a girl, and before she cracked a smile, the tunnel cracked his head.

Mark Maples wasn't a particularly close friend. But he was the first person I ever knew who died. He also was Disneyland's first-ever casualty, and his 1964 death on the Magic Kingdom's Matterhorn bobsleds became the stuff of legend. For me and my schoolmates it marked an end to innocence in the same place that, for many of us, it began: the Happiest Place on Earth.

Thinking about it now, I'm cognizant of a strange truth: Southern California is one of the few places on earth where childhood can begin and end at an amusement park.

It's hard to imagine the wondrous beacon of possibilities that Disneyland was for us back then, before youngsters could become heroic characters of their own choosing in intricate worlds of online fantasy. Think of an experience so special that you would literally dream of it for weeks before it happened, like a long-planned vacation or once-in-a-lifetime cruise. It's no exaggeration to say that for a kid growing up in my neighborhood five decades ago, this was the lofty status that the Magic Kingdom held.

Walt Disney himself predicted as much in his dedication at the park's opening day ceremonies in 1955. "To all who come to this happy place," he said, "welcome. Disneyland is *your* land. Here age relives fond memories of the past, and here youth may savor the challenge and promise of the future."

For me, the dream of childhood experienced a significant boost not too long after those words were uttered when my parents took me on a first visit. We'd just walked through the front entrance and were strolling across the town plaza when a train slid into the station and screeched to a halt. We turned in time to see a jaunty man with a cap pulled over his eyes jump from the engine and walk briskly toward the fire station.

My mother was the first to recognize the momentousness of the occasion. "Oh my goodness," she said in her thick German accent, "I think *det's* Mr. Disney."

Many years later I was to learn where he'd been headed in such a big hurry. By then I was a reporter for the *Los Angeles Times* doing a story on the tiny one-room apartment Disney secretly kept above the old-fashioned firehouse with its antique hook-and-ladder. Preserved exactly as he'd left it – but with a memorial candle now flickering in the window – the cozy unit looked out over the square on which the man affectionately referred to as "the boss" was said to have often gazed. For now, though, that knowledge was in the far-distant future and I was still a shy young boy about to sidle up to the larger-than-life deity whose famous visage graced his family's TV set every Friday.

"Let's go say hello," my father ordered, grabbing my arm. Before I could object, the park's dark-haired founder stood looking down upon us, as if from a great height. "Hello young man," Disney said in the grandfatherly voice so familiar that I felt like it was coming from my dreams. "What's your name? Are you enjoying the park?"

I have no idea how, or *if*, I responded. What I do remember is that Walt Disney hurriedly scribbled his name on a piece of paper we had proffered. It was the stub for an E-ticket ride. Had I kept it, I probably could one day have sold the thing and retired early.

For me, that day marks the start of a time when I learned to expect miracles. If a man I idolized on TV could suddenly jump off a train and shake my hand in the flesh, well, just about anything was possible. Perhaps, I began to believe, there really was some *magic* in the world. I still believe that. What *did* end, though, was my boundless childhood faith that magic can exist untarnished by reality.

That happened eight years later, on the day the bobsleds stopped.

Mark Maples was not particularly erudite or bright, and we had only a nodding acquaintance. But he had a ready smile and lots of friends at Stanford Junior High School where we were classmates. Like the rest of us, he also had a gaping vulnerability to Walt Disney's dream.

So it wasn't surprising to see him riding the Mad Hatter teacups with his girlfriend at our Disneyland Grad Night that spring. He waved at me, and I suppose I waved back. Two hours later I was in line for the Matterhorn bobsleds when suddenly they shut down. Gradually the news filtered back; something had happened, something bad.

By the next morning, we knew what it was.

I still think of Mark on lazy afternoons at Disneyland, when the delighted screams of bobsled riders waft through the summer air. On days like that I pull my young son closer in a silent prayer. Everyone's innocence must one day fade. My hope for him is that it won't happen too soon.

In my copy of the school yearbook bearing Mark's final portrait that June, I crossed out his name without leaving any comment. I think I sensed an important passage, but didn't know how to name it. Now, decades later, I see clearly what it was. Like bookends on a shelf, two events eight years apart marked childhood's symbolic beginning and its end. Though I didn't know it then, it was but the first of many beginnings and endings yet to come.

2.

Toking in a Trailer

The thing about my girlfriend that struck visitors right away was her habit of answering the door naked. Tina was an attractive young woman with a dazzling smile and long blonde hair wrapped in rainbow-colored ribbons, a girl who'd lived in San Francisco's Haight Ashbury in 1968, just one year before, and returned to spread the news. Occasionally I'd wrap my red beard in ribbons matching hers. Friends who came to the door of our Venice Beach apartment, however, hardly noticed *me* at all.

It wasn't just Tina's guest-greeting habits that set us apart. We were free, we'd tell anyone willing to listen, unbound by society's conventions. Sometimes we'd advertise that fact by strolling along the ocean boardwalk with other long-haired freaks wearing colored ribbons and tattered jeans. It was on one of these strolls that we passed an open door offering a startling glimpse into the future.

Through the entrance of Gold's Gym, we could see a dozen musclemen straining under the weight of their barbells. After a while, one of them noticed us and sauntered over. "How you doing?" asked Arnold Schwarzenegger in an accent that reminded me of my mother's. It was years, of course, before the accent would become famous and we'd learn his name. "*Vat* brings you here on *dis* beautiful day?"

And so we started chatting with this man from a different planet. The conversation was relaxed, but brief. He said he envied our "liberated" lifestyle. "You're lucky," he said, "because you're free."

But wasn't he enjoying his workouts, we wanted to know? "I don't recommend it unless you're a professional," Arnold declared. "It takes lots of discipline, and it's not too much fun."

Then he added something I didn't expect. "You're girlfriend's pretty," he said, "Do you mind if I pick her up?"

I was perplexed, but tried hard not to show it. "Hey, no problem," I said, wondering what in the world he was thinking. So the future governor of California picked Tina up as if she were a toothpick, hoisted her aloft like a human barbell and, as I held my breath, lifted her high above his head in several easy presses.

Holding herself rigid, she shrieked with delight. Then he spun her around, dropped her gently to her feet and, just like that, he was gone. A few years later we saw a movie called *Stay Hungry* and found out who Arnold was.

• • •

It's hard to explain how one transitions from honor student to hippie. At Long Beach Woodrow Wilson High School I'd earned good grades, served as Key Club president, got elected student Governor of Finance and played first-chair clarinet in the school orchestra. I'd even shown a mild inclination towards social activism by attending an interracial summer camp hosted by the National Conference of Christians and Jews and, later, organizing a tutoring service for "underprivileged" ghetto kids.

Then everything changed.

A couple of classmates – Les Thompson and Jimmie McFadden – joined with several other local musicians in 1966 to form a group called the Nitty Gritty Dirt Band that went on to record several major hits including "Mr. Bojangles." And a guy named Tony, whom I greatly admired, began treating me to weekly weed-smoking sessions aboard a hidden trailer in his backyard.

It's difficult to imagine nowadays what a revolutionary act that was. Possessing marijuana was a felony punishable by years in prison. So smoking a joint was seen as a courageous act of defiance, a statement proclaiming one's membership in the burgeoning underground of one's peers. It certainly wasn't something you did openly or talked about to anyone outside of that fraternity.

Some expressed their rebellion in more extreme and destructive ways. A high school friend named Michael Clark left home one Saturday night in 1965 with his father's high-powered rifle, parked himself on a hill overlooking Highway 101 and, early the next morning, started shooting at cars. The final toll was four dead, including Michael who blew his own brains out as police closed in. It was the first time any of us had ever heard of such a random act of violence, but certainly not the last.

Two other classmates, Michael Deeds and Chris Delance, became drug smugglers. A decade after high school, they sailed too close to the Cambodian coast on an Asian marijuana run and got picked up by soldiers of the murderous Pol Pot regime. Taken to Tuol Sleng Prison in Phnom Penh, the two were tortured for months and eventually executed, becoming the only Americans ever known to have died in that infamous place.

For most of us, though, the revolutionary '60s – at least in its earliest manifestations – meant embracing the things that our parents hated. But it was about more than just smoking dope. What it really constituted was a declaration of independence, not only from parents but from authority figures and the values we thought they represented. More importantly, it was about identifying with each other. We were fellow travelers who had long hair and knew the "secret handshake" by which to recognize our peers. Mostly it was about being outlaw siblings in what we perceived as a shining new outlaw world.

I have a handful of mental images still lingering from those heartfelt years. A naked young man standing amid a group of fellow frolickers on the beach with hands outstretched toward the sun. Dancing wildly at a free concert by the Doors in an upstairs parking lot at UCLA. I have another memory closer to home; of rising and falling in a pulsating ocean under psychedelic pink-tinged skies. What I didn't know then was that very soon the same ocean would be tinged with blood.

3.

Manson's Lawyer

They found Ronald Hughes' body wedged between two boulders in an ocean gorge. By then he'd been dead four months and was too decomposed for authorities to determine how he'd died. For those who knew him, though, there was never any doubt.

I'd first met Ron three years earlier in a class called *Non-Reality for Non Majors* that he was teaching at UCLA. He was a big man with a full red beard like mine and the look of an overpowering Teddy Bear. The course focused, basically, on how to openly demonstrate one's freedom by thumbing one's nose at society's traditional constraints; how, in other words, to act like a hippie. One way of doing that, Ron believed, was to take long playful frolics across campus sans clothes. Sometimes these excursions would end at the instructor's Westwood apartment where he'd encourage body painting and group massage. At other times they would conclude with a group skinny dip in the Inverted Fountain, a campus landmark near Franz Hall in which the water flowed down into a pit instead of up toward the sky.

During those romps, we'd often jog past a weekly ritual on campus. It was the Wednesday afternoon "silent vigil against the war," organized by philosophy professor Donald Kalish. Participating students would spend the lunch hour standing mute along Bruin Walk in silent testament to America's "sins" in Vietnam.

That tiny Southeast Asian country had been on my radar screen for a while by then, ever since Tony – the same guy who dispensed marijuana from his trailer and years later would die homeless and insane – sat me down in a school stairwell for a lecture on how the world worked. What was happening in Vietnam, he explained, was simple: they were good, we were bad. America, in other words, should mind its own business.

That analysis held some appeal; it was easy to understand, and easy to explain. And so began a long personal slide into leftist – and later *radical* – politics that would last for more than a decade. As a college freshman, though, I wasn't yet sure how to act on my newfound convictions. Walking past the silent vigil produced a definite tug of conscience. One Wednesday, shuffling down the walk fully clothed on a day that Ron's class had been canceled, I silently took my place behind the last guy in line. As I stood there, displaying political sentiments publically for the first time, I felt light-headed. But I also felt like I was home. And so my weekly routine changed; I dropped non-reality and started watching naked joggers from a perspective that was new.

• • •

Eventually I lost touch with Ron and his crew. Instead of hanging out with them, I started attending "teach-ins" on Vietnam. They were usually held at Meyerhoff Park, UCLA's designated free speech zone. One of the main targets was the Selective Service System which required males to carry draft cards from the age of 18. Sometimes protestors would burn their cards, vowing to resist military conscription. These were emotional affairs; young men, often with hands shaking, would light up the despised pieces of paper and hold them aloft like tiny sparklers for all to see. This was a federal offense; one could be – and often *was* – sent to prison for engaging in such self-indulgent acts of rebellion. I longed to follow their example, to be adored by my peers. At the very least, I was certain, they were getting way more sex than me. Even with that inducement, however, I could never muster the courage. So the draft card smoldered in my pocket while I, for the moment, remained a lowly spectator at the gates of change.

Sometimes the campus rallies took twists that were bizarre. One student decided to demonstrate the suffering of Vietnamese civilians by smearing napalm all over his forearm and lighting it with a match. As he moaned in agony trying to steady the smoking arm for our inspection, the sweetly nauseating smell of burning flesh made my guts churn.

Later I trembled with a surging sense of power as Eldridge Cleaver, an outspoken leader of the Black Panther Party, brought an entire assemblage to its feet at Pauley Pavilion chanting "Fuck Ronald Reagan." I had read Cleaver's book, *Soul on Ice,* and become a fan. Years later I sat down with him as a newspaper reporter to discuss his new book, *Soul on Fire,* written after he'd returned from exile in Algeria, helped bust Timothy Leary out of prison and, finally, become a born-again Christian.

"We fought the good fight," the former radical told me, looking back on that day at UCLA. "We did the best we could, but ideologically we were all wet. In the 1960s, black people were straddling the fence. We didn't want to go back to Africa, but we didn't want to be Americans either."

That dichotomy, not surprisingly, sometimes led to confusion on American campuses. Reporting for a black studies class one day, students were confronted by a yellow crime tape strung across the middle of the lecture hall guarded by several big Panthers in black berets. The famous African American poet, LeRoi Jones, we were told, was giving a reading and wanted to look out upon a sea of only black faces. So for the next hour, those of us with faces of a different hue – myself included – occupied the last two rows of the auditorium as

Jones spewed out a slew of angry words referring, among other things, to the "stench from the back of the room." One hothead objected and was immediately strong-armed out the door. The rest of us just kept quiet and listened, confident in the knowledge that we, at least, had scored sixteenth or seventeenth-row seats at the unfolding of events that were profound.

The day came, of course, when even that didn't seem adequate. One beautiful spring morning I watched in envy from the window of my U.S. history class as a group of African American students ceremoniously marched off campus burning American flags. "If you believe in justice," they chanted, "come with us. If you believe in equality, throw down your books." The flames of burning flags somehow seemed even more intoxicating than the glowing embers of sweltering draft cards, and I remember thinking how frustrating it was to be frozen in a classroom studying history while they were out there *making* it.

• • •

Then one night I saw Ronald Hughes, the master of non-reality, on TV. He was speaking into a microphone at a press conference regarding Charles Manson, the accused hippie cult murderer whose trial was then in full swing. When the anchor repeated Ron's name and title, I almost swallowed my spoon: my old UCLA teacher was Manson's lawyer!

I saw Ron only once after that. It was a few months later, as I stood in line for a Westwood movie on a visit to California from my new East Coast digs, and he happened by. The man had changed so much that I hardly recognized him. The laughing eyes had been replaced by slits that seemed to dart in every direction. On either side of him stood a beefy tattooed man who looked like a biker; clearly bodyguards. Ron stopped for a moment to say hello. "Hey David," he said, but the darting eyes made contact difficult. "How you doing, man?"

"Great," I said. "How about you?" We exchanged a few forced pleasantries, but it was obvious that he was uncomfortable. After about 15 seconds Ron said, "Good seeing you, man, I got to go," and disappeared into the wilds of Westwood.

Two weeks later he went missing and was never again seen alive.

Eventually we figured out what happened. Apparently Hughes had recently passed the bar, a fact he hadn't shared with many friends. He had never tried a case, though, so when Manson wanted to show contempt for the system prosecuting him, a neophyte lawyer must have seemed like the perfect choice with which to demonstrate his disdain. But the big bearded guy turned out to be smarter than the killer bargained for and the two never got along. Eventually someone else took the lead and the young "hippie lawyer," as he was called, began representing one of Manson's co-defendants, Leslie Van Houten.

In the waning days of the trial, Hughes attempted to separate his client's case from the cult leader's in the belief that she'd fare better alone. Manson, however, considered the move a threat to his authority for which he blamed Hughes. According to one account, on the last day of testimony the cult leader told the young lawyer that he never wanted to see him in court again and, indeed, he never did.

That weekend my old friend disappeared on a camping trip during a rainstorm in Topanga Canyon. Six weeks later – ironically on the same day the jury returned death penalties against all defendants – two fishermen found his remains in a gorge several miles away. Though the cause of death was never officially determined, at least one cult member later described it as Manson's final murder.

To Ron's friends and fellow travelers, the message was clear: what had begun as a naked traipse through the trees was no longer just a game. Innocent hippiedom was dead; now came the revolution. For the first of what would be a thousand times, I felt like returning to the house of my parents. I had not been there in a while, had not even spoken to them of my emerging new purpose. Yet that was where I'd come into this scary and bewildering world, the entry point separating the present from the magic that was childhood. I could use some of that magic now. And so I thought of the day my father summoned earthworms.

4.

Worms

The moment of truth came when they started slithering up through holes in the ground. There were hundreds of them, occupying every inch of the yard, burrowing up through the grass to wiggle helplessly on the green shiny lawn; more slimy orange earthworms than we had ever seen. "You see," my father said triumphantly, "here they are and here they come."

For him it was a perfect moment involving incredulous children with large bulging eyes. The children were me and my friends, practically every kid in the neighborhood. And what we were seeing was my father's latest invention.

As long as I could remember, he'd been an amateur inventor. It had begun years earlier when he was an electrical engineer at Raytheon, a major defense contractor with offices on Terminal Island near Long Beach, California. Dad slept very little, preferring to spend his nights tinkering at the workbench he'd assembled in the garage. Then, just about the time we'd start forgetting who he was, he'd clamor into the kitchen with some new contraption from Oz.

Once it was a weird corrugated metal panel that he mounted on the patio roof and, after stringing its narrow gullies with garden hose, claimed that water circulating through the black hose would magically heat up our pool. Though none of us ever felt any appreciable increase in the temperature as we swam, we were duely impressed with dad's theoretical ingenuity. It would be decades, of course, before any of us

– or anyone we knew, for that matter – would hear of a new-fangled concept called solar energy.

Another time he built a little electronic wooden oven that he called a radar range. Its best feature, he said, was that it could cook hamburgers in less than three minutes without using flames. To prove it, dad organized a luau for a Sunday afternoon and invited all the neighbors. To this day, one of the most enduring images of my childhood is him wearing a chef's hat and Hawaiian lei flipping backyard burgers to a hungry wide-eyed crowd. I have often wondered how many of them eventually got cancer from this unprotected exposure to an early prototype of what we now know as the microwave oven. By the time that would have happened, of course, my father – always a man of science rather than sense – would have long since moved on.

Then he got interested in earthworms.

. . .

If you ran an electric current through the earth they occupied, he discovered, they'd hightail it up toward sunlight to escape the electrified ground. So dad hooked up an old hand-cranked military field generator to two metal poles, inserted one into each end of the lawn and, varoom, in short order our front yard had become earthworm city! While the technique may have been known to others, to us kids it was a revelation. The challenge, of course, was finding a practical use for the procedure. But dad had no interest in fishing, so the whole apparatus eventually went the way of its predecessors; onto a dusty shelf in the garage.

People said the source of my father's eccentricity was his mother. A feminist before the term was coined, she had left her husband while Dad was still in the womb and then, eschewing a series of suitors to remain single in the early decades of the century, retreated to a remote

Cheyenne Indian reservation in Montana to teach English and give birth to her son.

He spent much of his youth at the Voorhees School for Boys, a program for youngsters from "broken homes" in San Dimas, California, while she gallivanted through southern Mexico doing whatever liberated women did in the days before women were liberated. The school's founder and headmaster was Jerry Voorhees, an avowed socialist who later became a Democratic U.S. Congressman famous for his 1946 defeat by Richard M. Nixon in the future president's first bid for public office. I still have childhood memories of attending the school's reunions at a park near the old campus where Voorhees – then already an elderly pundit and statesman – fondly held court with his still-adoring "boys."

My father's own political tendencies also leaned decidedly towards the left, a fact that got him into trouble during the McCarthy period of the 1950s. By then he was a 20-something merchant seaman radio operator first class and active union organizer who, by his own admission, had attended several meetings of the American Communist Party. So when he tried to renew his seaman's license at the same time that U.S. Senator Joseph McCarthy was famously looking for communists in every coffee can, well, he ran into problems.

Eventually Dad was cleared, but the affair left some serious scars: paranoia regarding any action taken by the government, deep fears about expressing divergent views and the strong admonition to his children to "never sign your name." Then he forgot the Morse code.

It happened one day on a cruise to Alaska when Dad, in his early sixties, simply went blank. The captain promptly put him ashore at the next port and my poor progenitor had to make his way home. I'll never forget his pathetic call from the airport. "I need you to pick me up," he said, sounding more depressed than I'd ever heard him. "I can't go to sea anymore."

The next decade was shrouded in darkness as my father sank slowly into the tar pit of Alzheimer's. I don't remember much of those early years. What I do remember are the days near the end when our only defense was humor. Once he walked out the front door of his house, ostensibly to borrow milk from a neighbor, and just kept walking. We found him hours and miles later sporting crusted lips and a sweating brow. Another time he fell through an upstairs wall the night before our house went up for sale. So the next morning potential buyers were treated to the cartoonish sight of a wall with a hole in it exactly the shape of my dad.

When the end finally came in 1989, I was at a San Fernando Valley park covering the gathering of a group called Skinheads Against Racism, an organization desperately trying to change the Nazi-like image of skinheads. Returning home late that night, I saw the lights on with several relatives waiting in the driveway and immediately knew what had happened.

The last time I saw Dad alive, he was lying in his bed at the terrible nursing home to which he'd been consigned when we could no longer care for him ourselves. I had managed to drop by for a few minutes after work but, as usual, couldn't tell whether he even recognized me. Then suddenly, as sometimes happens with Alzheimer's patients, the clouds parted and he had a moment of clarity. Dad smiled and, in the hoarse voice that had become his own, asked a very important question.

"Do you think I'm getting better?"

I smiled back and, with a heart full of sadness, tried to answer as best I could. "At moments like this," I said, "I *know* that you are."

Then he leaned forward to beckon me close. As the darkness hovered just outside our perimeters threatening to snatch him back into its embrace, my father struggled to hold onto his thoughts. Putting his lips close, he whispered in my ear. "Never sign your name," he said, and the darkness closed in.

It was a pervasive darkness that had grown familiar, the universal echo chamber of gloom I hoped to one day penetrate. It was the same darkness in which, by then, I had spent many years searching for a point of light.

David Haldane

5.

Politico

A movie about the Cuban revolution had just ended when a man in the front row screamed. It was a piercing scream, the kind you'd expect from a girl, and it bounced off the walls of the campus auditorium like a ricocheting bullet that punched an icy hole in my heart. Suddenly he jumped off his seat as if it were electrified and bolted straight for a wall. Five women quickly followed as a sixth sauntered up to the stage.

"Sisters and brothers," she announced in a tone that seemed rehearsed, "this man is a pig. What you are about to witness is revolutionary justice."

As the women closed in on him, the man's hands crawled up the wall like spiders scrambling to safety. When the hands reached their zenith, they stopped and only the fingers kept moving; scratching, probing, frantically gouging. Then the women beat the crap out of him as my punctured heart stopped and the people around me ejected audible gasps. Something new had entered our lives, something they called *feminism*. Only it wasn't your mother's brand of feminism. This was a more radical variety, the kind that burst onto the scene in 1969 in an explosion of frustrations that had simmered for years. And like all the other isms of the era, it had reached its boiling point at a time when inhibitions were forbidden and explosions were the norm.

By then I had transferred to Goddard College, a small rustic campus and former Unitarian seminary on what had once been a farm in rural Vermont. Known as "progressive," the college was far different from UCLA which was structured, complex and stock full of rules. Life at Goddard, which had only 500 students, was simple; you did what you wanted and learned what you could. And what most people wanted to learn was how to make revolution. The major social event of the week was the Saturday night movie in the campus auditorium – a vast wooden structure called the Hay Barn – and it was there that Goddard's first victim of radical feminism got his due. We never learned the particulars of his offense, only that he was allegedly a seducer of young women, someone who today might be dubbed a sexual predator.

To the rest of us the message was clear: beware of what you do or what you say because there could be a terrible price to pay. For the unfortunate man with the spidery hands it was already too late; within a week he had transferred to another, perhaps less treacherous, campus far away. For me, though, it was a glimpse of what was to come. I had enrolled at Goddard in pursuit of Tina, the blonde-haired nature child from Venice who had transferred here before me. What I found instead was a ringside seat to the transformation of a culture.

This was readily apparent on the first day of registration, when I'd been given the choice of living in the vegetarian, revolutionary or nudist dorm. My initial inclination, of course, was to go naked, but I managed to resist that impulse and, instead, opted to live with the politicos. The impression of libertine weirdness deepened the next day when the bearded college president canceled classes for a week in favor of a "Dionysian Festival" featuring food, flutes, flowers and wine. It virtually punched me in the eye and took no prisoners, though, several days later when I was awakened at 5 a.m. by a clamor outside.

Peering through my dorm-room window, I was utterly transfixed by the strange spectacle of 50 young people armed with football helmets and baseball bats glaring at each other across an open field.

Suddenly a guy who seemed to be their leader blew a whistle and the two sides charged forward with bats in full swing. Thirty seconds later it was all over; a writhing ocean of groaning bodies lay strewn across the grass. "Excellent!" the leader observed, "now let's do it again."

Perhaps, it occurred to me in passing, this was the "non-reality" for which the dead Ronald Hughes had been preparing.

What I was watching, I soon learned, were the antics of the Weathermen; a new quasi-terrorist antiwar group planning to "bring the Vietnam War home." Their strategy: to gather on the streets of Chicago, scene of the raucous Democratic National Convention the year before, in two weeks for a massive protest dubbed Days of Rage. One of the group's leaders, a Goddard student named Russell Neufeld, had brought the Boston contingent up to Vermont to whip it into shape. And the best way to do that, he apparently believed, was to encourage its members to beat each other senseless with clubs.

This was not the first political event I'd witnessed in Vermont. A few weeks earlier, I'd sat in the Burlington living room of a self-proclaimed socialist named Bernie Sanders as he watched himself on TV for the first time in his very first bid for public offfice. The event was a pre-taped debate between him and several other candidates for U.S. Senate, an office the neophyte politician coveted but hardly seemed likely to win.

"Oh my God," the disheveled mop-haired wannabe had screamed at his own image on the screen. "This guy looks an idiot. I would never vote for a bum like that!"

Decades later, Sanders – whose political career had begun at Goddard with the founding of an independent leftist party called Liberty Union – would indeed become the venerable senator from Vermont following literally dozens of unsuccessful tries. The only avowed socialist in the U.S. Congress, he eventually emerged as a strong contender for the 2016 Democratic presidential nomination whose moniker would become a household name.

Having the Weathermen on campus, though, was decidedly different. They stayed for a week, during which the rest of us marveled and trembled at their antics. My favorite: the arrest of one of them – perhaps it was Neufeld – walking out of the local general store with several pairs of long johns under his jeans. "We requisition these for the revolution!" he'd screamed as police led him away. The question of the hour: Would this young would-be revolutionary be liberated in time for action or sit out Days of Rage in the Plainfield jail? I never learned the answer.

On the day of the great event, those of us who had stayed in Vermont sat glued to a TV set in our dorm lobby breathlessly awaiting the show. Most of us were rooting for the Weathermen. For, in truth, while there was plenty about them to laugh at, there was also something gnawingly admirable. In a word, it was their courage; in a placid sea of discourse and theory, the Weathermen were a great whooshing fireball of energy, a comet of change streaking through our lives. "Are you for real?" they demanded. "Do you mean what you say or are you just playing games?"

We'd heard rumors that, to hide their identities, the Goddard contingent had stolen dozens of student IDs before departing for Chicago. None of us fully appreciated the significance of that, however, until, sitting at the edges of our seats, we learned that 350 demonstrators had stormed the streets of Chicago smashing the windows of automobiles, businesses and homes.

"One protester has been shot," a TV newsman announced, describing the police counterattack that had beaten back the throng. "Authorities have tentatively identified him as 23-year-old Marshall Berzan of Vermont."

Suddenly there was a commotion in the seat next to mine. Turning white and visibly shaken, the *real* Marshall Berzan stood up and promptly left the room, presumably to call his parents and report that he was alive. Reading a history of the event years later, I was stunned to learn that he was listed as the first casualty of Days of Rage.

So much for history. And so much for watching it from the sidelines.

6.

Baseball Bats

A lot of what happened next had to do with baseball bats. Though quintessential symbols of American sportsmanship and leisure, they can also be used for less noble purposes. We had seen an example of that during the Weatherman clubbing fest at Goddard College. Very soon now, my own head would tempt a bat. And due to the intercession of several undisciplined baseball bats, a friend would be transformed from a smart-looking military cadet into a bloody unconscious mass crumpled in a heap beneath his bed.

In truth, it was partly my fault. It had started as a simple idea, really. A few of us thought that we could talk some sense into the heads of the war-crazed cadets at Norwich University, the country's oldest – and one of its most prestigious – military academies not too far from Goddard College. How hard could it be, we reasoned? Opposition to the war wasn't rocket science. As my childhood chum had taught me, it was simply a matter of good (the Vietcong) versus evil (the U.S. military), and who in his right mind would willingly fight on the side of evil?

Back in 1861 – some 40 years after its founding – this cradle of the ROTC in Norwich, Vermont, was training officers to fight for preservation of the union. So in 1969 we decided to invade the campus with huge brightly-painted signs attesting to the futility of war. Our theory: that the confused and misguided cadets would read them, recognize the wisdom of their words, and immediately quit school to join the side of the angels. Instead, a group of them grabbed baseball bats and surrounded us, quite appropriately, on an athletic field near third base.

For a moment, I must admit, I thought we were about to lose the argument. Then salvation arrived, ironically, in the form of a uniformed military officer who ordered them to put down their sticks while we made our escape.

A few days later we were back, this time in an auditorium full of scowling militarists busting for a fight, courtesy of the same officer who had just saved our lives. "We called this assembly," he told them, "so that some, um, anti-war protestors from Goddard could come over and, well, *introduce* themselves." As the cadets hissed, I seriously wondered whether the convener of this gathering really wanted to encourage dialogue, as he had alleged, or was simply a frustrated humorist trying for a bit of irony. Perhaps, it occurred to me, he had reconsidered his earlier protective action at the baseball field, realized it was a mistake and decided to undo it here and now.

"OK," he said, almost as an afterthought as a man with a crew cut and camera stood up in the first row. "Let's at least give these people a listen."

Fifteen minutes later a fellow anti-warrior named James, with hair practically down to his butt, was explaining to 50 uniformed Norwich cadets why they should renounce war when one of them jumped to his feet. "My fuckin' brother *died* in Vietnam," he said with eyes bulging and red veins popping from his neck. "Are you telling me he died for nothing?"

"That's *exactly* what I'm telling you!" James shot back, and the silence was so gaseous that I feared they could hear me gulp. Then all hell broke loose and the photographer, apparently an academy employee, moved in to get profiles and close-ups as, for the second time in a week, we beat a hasty retreat. It was with some trepidation, therefore, that, approaching the steps to my dorm less than an hour later, I saw several cadets in civilian clothes who apparently had gotten there ahead of me.

"Hey hippie," one of them said as I passed. I stopped cold and stared at him, ready to take off. To my amazement, he was smiling. "Hey soldier boy," I said. The cadet stood up, slapped me on the back and handed me a beer. "Relax," he said, "and let's have a talk."

His name was Richard and he said that he was looking for help. "Can you get these guys out of the draft?" Richard wanted to know. I glanced at the circle of his friends, assaulted by hopeful, penetrating stares all around. "You guys are kind of already *in* the military," I said, "Are you serious?"

There was a long silence as they contemplated the question. Then Richard took a sip of his beer and smiled broadly. "Hell no," he said. "We're here for the chicks."

As I got to know him over the next several weeks, however, I came to realize that there were certain things about which Richard was *deadly* serious. The scion of a military family from New York, he had dabbled in leftist politics without ever "coming out." Now, following the dictates of his father, he found himself in the hills of Vermont disguised as a Norwich cadet. And he was miserable. His life, Richard said, was patterned like the lines of a grid, filled with painted barriers he could not cross and mental leaps he could not make. Almost every moment of his existence was scripted, he felt, and nearly everything desirable proscribed.

For a long time Richard had managed to suck it up and keep his mouth shut. But the world outside was changing, increasingly resembling his geography within. He no longer believed in the war. And our appearance at Norwich, he said, had confirmed that even in his most subversive thoughts he wasn't alone. And so, as his fellow cadets heckled us, Richard had sat there silently hatching a plan.

In three weeks, U.S. Secretary of Defense Robert McNamara was scheduled to deliver the Norwich commencement address. As a member of the graduating class, Richard would be there. His idea: stage a one-man walkout to let his position be known. At any normal American university, mind you, a walkout by one student would hardly be noticed. But Norwich was hardly normal. Here such a thing would constitute a serious breach of discipline and protocol. And to walk out on McNamara with news cameras blazing, well, something like that was simply unthinkable. But Richard said he wanted to do it, and so we decided to help.

Two weeks before the momentous occasion, I made my third and final foray to the Norwich wilds to secretly deliver a stack of antiwar leaflets to his room. The plan was for him to distribute them as he walked out of the auditorium. Arriving with the papers tucked neatly under my shirt, however, it felt more like I was delivering drugs.

"You got the stuff?" he asked after covertly ushering me in.

"Yeah right here," I said, pulling out the stack and tossing it onto the bed.

"All right," he said. "You better split before my roommate gets back."

I turned to leave, but suddenly he grabbed my arm. "Wait a minute," he said. Richard went to the dresser, opened its top drawer and pulled out a khaki-colored beret. "Wear this," he ordered.

"What the hell for?"

He looked at me like I was one of his plebes. "Obviously," he said, "it's to hide your long hair." But there would be no hiding from the chaos to come.

. . .

We never found out how they got on to him. For weeks we'd been holding secret meetings in private apartments throughout Vermont, Richard, me and a few Goddard activists. Our plan was to stage a demonstration just off campus which Richard would join after doing his thing in the auditorium. For him it would undoubtedly spell the end of any hopes for a military career. For Norwich, we trusted, the beginning of a new consciousness.

At first everyone felt optimistic, especially Richard. He would always enter the room smiling, clasping hands with brotherly affection. His joy was contagious as if the revolution had already been won with the liberation of just one soul.

After my final visit to Norwich, however, things started tensing up. One day Richard walked in with a scowl on his face. "They got wind of it," he said falling into his chair.

"Who did?" I asked.

"The provost," he said, "who the fuck else?"

Over the next several days, an ominous dark cloud seemed to be gathering around him. Richard was told that two "friends" would be seated next to him in the auditorium to prevent him from "doing anything foolish." Mysterious threats against his physical well-being began appearing on lavatory walls. And all but his staunchest friends were suddenly afraid to be seen with him.

Despite everything, he was determined to go ahead. The last time I saw Richard he looked pensive; it was a week before commencement and somehow he'd managed to sneak off campus. But he wouldn't be able to do it again, he assured us, so any last minute details had to be planned. "Whatever happens," he promised, "I won't back down."

Three days later his roommate found him unconscious under the bed next to one of the bloody baseball bats that had beat in his head. Though Richard was alive, he was seriously injured. If there was a silver lining, it was that he had finally found a way out of Norwich, though I never learned where he finally ended up.

• • •

It was partly in Richard's honor that I volunteered to act as a local coordinator for an upcoming action in Washington D.C. It promised to be the biggest antiwar demonstration any of us had ever seen, an event of truly national proportions. Organized by the Vietnam Moratorium Committee, the massive protest – scheduled for Nov. 15, 1969 – was intended to be nonviolent. But Days of Rage, while falling far short of its participants' expectations, had succeeded in introducing a new level of unpredictability to the antiwar movement. So after trekking to the nation's capital in a chartered bus overstuffed with fellow protestors, I felt compelled to offer some words of encouragement to the Goddard contingent before letting them loose on the street."Uh, we don't know what's going to happen out there today," I stammered, praying that I didn't sound as stupid as I felt. "We've heard about potentially violent provocateurs."

Here I paused for effect.

"So if the shit hits the fan," I concluded with solemn profundity, "well, let's just try to be cool."

My speech was over. I didn't know what else to say. Left unspoken, of course, was the feeling we all shared, that this undertaking would be historic. That if you needed a student loan, in other words, you shouldn't hesitate to get it because the revolution would be over before the money came due.

For me the "shit hit the fan" just hours later when, caught in the chaos of a decomposing situation, I found myself standing in back of a police line staring at an imposing building. The demonstration had started out well. Tens of thousands of protestors, virtually packing the streets of Washington like ants carrying crumbs, marched in neat lines chanting antiwar slogans and waving signs saying "PEACE" and "End the War Now!"

Years later, the *New York Times* would describe that day's events as "the largest antiwar protest in U.S. history" with more than half-a-million participants. Among those addressing the crowd were U.S.

Nazis and Nudists

Senators Eugene McCarthy and George McGovern, past and future presidential candidates respectively, with musical performances by Peter, Paul and Mary, Arlo Guthrie and Pete Seeger, who led the crowd in singing John Lennon's "Give Peace a Chance."

Only a few hours later, though, the fringes of the crowd grew ugly. That's when, standing behind the police line, I suddenly heard a loud clamor from the back and, turning, felt my bowels turn to mush. A helmeted group of what I took to be Weathermen was advancing with bats in their hands and fire in their eyes. The police whirled around with ice in theirs. And as they pulled their gas masks down over those frozen orbs, the full weight of my predicament suddenly became clear; I was caught between opposing armies. I made it to the sidewalk just in time to hear the hiss of teargas grenades hitting the street as I pressed my face into the wall looking frantically for a crack.

"Taste this motherfuckers!" one of the cops yelled, and so I did.

It didn't taste good. It tasted so bad, in fact, that my eyes swelled shut and something like pus oozed out from every pore. My face felt like a soggy pin cushion. I took a handkerchief from my pocket and held it over my eyes, but to no avail. Slowly making my way back to where I estimated the bus to be, I was vaguely aware of the flash of cameras as I walked past the shadowy line of cops silently watching me like ghosts. I wondered whether one of them might be wielded by the same photographer who had been at Norwich. For the next several days, I could see nothing but the insides of my eyelids. A perfect place from which to contemplate the sound of the voices that I would soon hear.

7.

Whispers in a Graveyard

I was kneeling in a cemetery when the voices first spoke. Though I didn't yet realize it, I was about to experience an even more direct encounter with the God behind my eyes.

The old graveyard was a spot on the Goddard campus dating back to a time when the place was called Kate's Farm, far from any classroom and known only to those willing to take long treks through meadow and wood. One Sunday afternoon I did just that. It wasn't a typical Sunday, though. On this particular day I finally took a friend's advice to swallow one of the little pills he called mescaline.

For those too young to remember, mescaline was one of the less appreciated psychedelic drugs of the 1960s and early '70s Though never achieving the overarching fame and glory of its bigger sister, LSD, it was every bit the hallucinogen of its more venerated sibling and, by any reasonable standard, not to be taken lightly.

It also had a long and noble history, existing naturally in the peyote cactus plants found extensively throughout the Americas. Ingested in that form, the substance had played a key role in the religious rituals performed for more than 5,700 years by the Native Americans of Mexico and, later, the U.S. They claimed that the cactus induced visions of the spiritual world and evoked a sense of oneness with the earth and all life forms. Many also believed that the plant enabled communion with spirits, a deeply moving experience described, among others, by Aldous Huxley, Hunter S. Thompson and, most famously, Carlos Castaneda in several bestselling novels.

I, of course, had read some of those accounts and was eager to partake. Ah, but how to explain the difference? Let me try by saying simply: if LSD is red, then mescaline is blue. If LSD grabs you by the short hairs for a thrilling rollercoaster ride through lollipop skies, mescaline massages your eyeballs with the gentler undulations of that sky's more subtle colors.

And so it began; a psychic journey that would carve a new synapse in an otherwise virginal brain. The first remarkable thing I noticed was that the clouds resembled mother-of-pearl, as if seen through a wave of heat, both in substance and in color. One minute I was walking through a meadow of tall grass that was waving to me happily and the next, well, there I was at the cemetery's gate.

I have seen many memorable cemeteries in my time. In Southern California there's one hidden near Mission San Juan Capistrano shielding the remains of the city's missionary founders as well as the Native Americans they managed to convert. And many years later, I would visit a graveyard near Manila that doubled as a shanty squatter's town. None of them, however, affected me more than the ancient tombstones planted in tidy little rows at Kate's Farm. Even as I approached, I could hear them talking amongst themselves. Let me revise that: I could *feel* them talking.

"He's afraid," one particularly opinionated tombstone was saying. "Look at the way he walks, the doubt in his eyes..." There was a pause as its neighbor considered how to reply. "He is afraid because he thinks he's better than us," the second tombstone finally said. "Imagine the arrogance of feeling superior simply because you're alive."

That's when I understood that it wasn't the *tombstones* I was hearing, but the spirits beneath them. I decided to pay close attention to what they were saying and, for the next several hours, was amply rewarded. To a casual observer, I'm sure, the scene would have looked bizarre: a deteriorating old cemetery deserted save for a long-haired young man in torn jeans kneeling carefully before each grave. To that young man, though, the encounter seemed fraught with life-changing significance.

As each grave spoke in turn, a consistent theme began to emerge. Death, they were saying, is nothing but a thin veneer; on one side are the ageless dead millions who can clearly see the divide while on the other stand those who, like me, yet breathe and still fear the crossing. The main topic of discussion: the extraordinary lengths to which the living will go to avoid that ethereal curtain, ignore it, diminish its significance or explain it away. To the living, in other words, death seems like a major chasm to breach and a hurdle to overcome.

"They are weak," one spirit said. "They live in so much fear."

"If only they could see what we see," another said. "Such a shame that truth is reserved for the dead."

Later as I sauntered home from that graveyard through the ancient meadows of Vermont, I felt as if an angel had alighted on my shoulder: light and breezy with a smiling heart, it made my skin tingle and my mind soar. Feeling a deep-seated joy, I stopped to lie in the grass and stare up at the pulsating mother-of-pearl sky. And that's where, eight hours after my journey began, my friends found me resting on green leaves laughing hysterically that death didn't exist.

In fairly short order, of course, the euphoria passed and the feeling faded with the effects of the drug. In retrospect, though, that afternoon was a turning point, the beginning of a search that was to dominate and define – even if unconsciously – many of the ensuing years. Simply put, it was a search for that lost and elusive green leafy space. Somehow I knew that one day I would find it. First, though, there was the little matter of a few dozen Maoists to beat up.

8.

Each According to His Need

The truth is that I hadn't meant to draw blood. The problem was that the guy's head kept hitting my fist. Don't get me wrong, I'm not normally a violent person. But this wasn't normal. This was revolutionary war. And, as in any war, the rules of engagement had changed.

The day had started, innocently enough, with an early-morning call. "Good morning comrade," the Organizer said, "we need you at Columbia University in half an hour." And so began my stint as a revolutionary attack dog.

They come in many breeds. I had first encountered *my* breed – the Trotskyist Young Socialist Alliance – in the woods of Vermont not too long after communing with those spirits. The canine I met sat me down for a talk. "If you're serious about changing this country," he said, "come to New York City." So I took a long break from college, rented an apartment, and here I was. I had turned 22 and the world lay at my feet.

The problem at Columbia, we were told upon arrival, was that the Maoists were taking over. They were a competing breed that we officially hated and a wild pack of them was on its way. Their aim, we quickly learned, was to rip apart a peaceful student antiwar protest in an effort to gain control. Ours: to thwart that attempt and exert our own.

As the students held their rally, we linked arms forming a

protective barrier around them. For a while nothing happened. Then, as advertised, the Maoists attacked. For the record, they were members of a group called the Progressive Labor Party committed to the teachings of Mao Tse-tung who, as any student of history knows, was the communist leader of what was then called Red China said to be responsible for millions of deaths. We, on the other hand, were followers of Leon Trotsky, a leader of the Russian Revolution who'd been exiled by Joseph Stalin and murdered with an ice pick in 1940.

Bottom line: we held the higher moral ground. Which is why we had no qualms about beating the crap out of a bunch of snarling Maoists. It was the first time I had ever directly participated in political violence.

A word here about radicalism: it sneaks up behind you. At first you just glance over your shoulder. You say to yourself that you're a curious person who wants to know what's going on. Then you start getting some ideas and perhaps even begin nodding a little in your sleep. But you're still cool; you're not about to do anything crazy or take any real risks. So you keep your distance and tell your friends not to worry. But one day radicalism passes you in the street and you feel your heart leap. And that's when you know that you're lost.

The appeal of Trotskyism, I think, was that it made me feel found. In an ocean of chaos and conflicting ideologies, here was one that seemed solid. More importantly, in a world populated by people uncertain of what to do, the Trotskyists always had a plan. It was as if, thrown into a stormy sea after the shipwreck of my previous assumptions, I had found a raft to keep me afloat.

But how does one make the ideological leap from opposing the actions of one's government to openly opposing the economic system that informs them? Not to worry, the YSA leadership proclaimed. The Vietnam War, they explained, was a "transitional" issue much like the tip of an iceberg. If you started with what's visible and followed it to its source, there was only one place you could arrive. Because they believed capitalism to be the source of war and all other evils, that place would be socialism. And so they drew me in. Despite the to-each-according-to-his-needs ideology, however, being a socialist didn't pay the bills. So I became a cab driver too.

The job wasn't bad. After reporting to work at 4 p.m., I'd cruise the city all night free to think my own thoughts between fares. It felt like a private parallel universe. Then morning would arrive, and I'd park the cab before making my way back to YSA headquarters. That too offered a parallel universe of sorts, but one of a completely different hue. In that universe I was a political drone: a guy who read books, attended meetings, wrote pamphlets and publically proselytized about the revolution to come.

One day my efforts were rewarded with a cushy assignment: accompanying Kipp Dawson, a socialist candidate for U.S. Senator from New York, on a statewide campaign tour. Her job: spreading the party's platform. Mine: doing all the grunt work to make that possible. We made lots of stops, including one at a Catholic girls' school in Poughkeepsie, New York.

We also dropped in to visit a comrade at Vassar College who had incurred the wrath of party leaders by allegedly proclaiming her lesbianism, a sexual orientation then strictly forbidden by YSA rules. Kipp's mission was to ascertain whether it was true and, if so, whip her into line. I, unfortunately, was barred from that meeting for the far more serious offense of possessing a penis which, apparently, was strictly forbidden by *lesbian* rules. Less than a year later, the YSA would reverse its position on homosexuality and some of its most visible leaders admit that they'd been gay all along.

The highlight of the trip for me, though, was our appearance on an Albany radio station that touted the show as an *Expose': Albany Infiltrated by Communists*!! "So," the host asked me during a lull in calls, "I understand you're a new recruit. How far along are *you* in the brainwashing process?"

That was my cue. I cleared my throat. "First of all," I said, "I object to your use of the term *brainwashing*. Socialists don't brainwash anybody, everything is discussed openly. I'm not here because I was brainwashed, but because I saw a need for change in this society and acted on that perception." Kipp silently mouthed the word "*perfect,*" giving me a highball sign unseen by the host. I had learned my lines well.

My perception of the YSA began to change a few weeks later when the organization mobilized for a national antiwar convention in Cleveland, Ohio, aimed at setting the movement's agenda for the coming year. Hundreds of us were transported in buses to the convention hall, where we were immediately escorted into a caucus meeting and instructed how to vote. For me it was a lesson in the power of political organization and the manipulation of democracy; as the YSA wished, so the convention went.

. . .

I thought about that the next time I guided my cab through darkened city streets, wondering whether these activists were really the people in whose country I wanted to live. I was probably thinking about it the night I realized that there was a gun pointed at my head.

The question was whether the man was going to shoot me. My best guess was that he probably would. And yet I felt strangely removed from the prospect of my own death. It was as if it was happening to someone else and I was simply observing. Perhaps, it fleetingly occurred to me, this was due to the lingering legacy of that graveyard in Vermont with its green leafy space.

New York City hardly seemed a likely place to find the peace I was seeking. But I was mesmerized by the city with all its strange lights and grid-like veins. Sometimes between fares I would allow myself to be drawn into them, imagining that I was speeding with the city's bloodstream towards its very heart. Where that was, exactly, was hard to say: Columbia Circle, Central Park, Times Square? Perhaps, I grandiosely imagined, it was wherever I was, sitting next to me in my cab.

I loved working nights. There was a magic to it, a feeling of freedom and otherworldliness that made me sit up straight. The nighttime lights of the city threw a yellowish sheen onto the dashboard that put me into an altered state of consciousness, a parallel universe full of visions and surprises. The people entering that space, even just for a while, added to the sense of strangeness; among them were coke sniffers looking for hits, prostitutes with johns in tow and illicit couples making furtive love in the privacy that only a backseat can afford.

One night a morbidly obese man wearing tent-sized gray pants and sandals the size of my head clamored into that backseat with a lithe young woman in a tight-fitting skirt. Breathing heavily, he tightly held her knee as we swept down Park Avenue playing tag with the lights. Suddenly he ordered me stop at the corner of 57th and pecked her on the cheek of an expressionless face as she quickly hopped out.

"You're lucky," he said mournfully as we regained speed. "You don't have to pay somebody to be with you. You'll never know what that's like."

Another time I picked up a teenager, perhaps 17, with a furtive look on his ruddy face. "Where you going?" I gamely inquired.

"I don't know," he said without pausing to catch his breath. "Anywhere that's far away from here."

A few blocks later I got pulled over by the cops who informed me that my passenger's parents wanted him back. I remember it well because he exchanged my cab for their squad car and I never got paid.

Then some of the luster of this new adventure, too, began to fade. Rushing a visiting Italian couple to JFK one night, I landed them at the curb just short of the deadline for check-in. But the trunk got stuck, locking their luggage inside. In 20 minutes, after failing at everything else, I managed to pry it open with a borrowed crowbar but still wasn't able to get them to the counter in time. Inexplicably, they gave me a $30 tip nonetheless. In the end, though, it didn't matter because several hours later, the tip – along with the rest of the night's earnings – disappeared into the pockets of four guys who got into my cab wielding knives.

"All right, Jack," one of them said, holding the blade to my throat as I handed him my cigar box full of bills. I still remember the green paper fluttering in the wind as the robbers made their mad escape.

Finally the night came when I picked up that skanky couple at Times Square. Having just returned from the disillusioning antiwar convention in Cleveland, I'd been mentally wrestling with all its implications. Almost immediately the couple started making out in the backseat as I watched uneasily through the rear view mirror. When we passed a toll booth, the man told me to pay and that he would later reimburse. Then, about half way down the Long Island Expressway, something poked me in the back of the head.

"Hey motherfucker," the guy said, "That's a gun. Do exactly as I say or I'll blow out your brains."

Honestly, it felt like I was in a movie. He had me hand over the cigar box, and my wallet too. Then ordered me to stop the car and get out by the side of the road. "Lie on your belly next to the front wheel," the man growled. He got out of the back seat, stepped over me, slid into the front and slammed the door shut. From the corner of my eye, I could see him sitting on the passenger's side, grinning cruelly with the gun pointing at me like a bulldog's snout. I felt him wavering. Finally he spoke. "I ought to blow your brains out you honkey fool." Then he slid into the driver's seat, gunned the engine and took off with the rear tire missing my head by an inch.

A couple of cops showed up to take a report. I told them the story, and they told me good luck. Hitching back to Manhattan to tell my boss that I'd lost his cab was one of the hardest things I'd ever done. Fortunately a carload of hippies picked me up, so by the time I got to the garage I was thoroughly stoned.

"Uh, something kind of bad happened," I began.

The boss looked thoroughly disgusted, but not at all surprised. It was the last time I ever saw him. Three days later I was back at the airport embarked on a journey that would shake my soul. In truth, I was just happy to still have one to shake.

David Haldane

9.

Chillin' with a Chillum

Had an East German border guard been slightly more diligent, that poor battered soul might have languished in prison for years. "*Achtung achtung!*" the guard shouted boarding my train sounding, I swear, exactly like a Nazi. "*Ausweiss bitte*, passport please!"

Without even thinking, I knew that I was fucked.

Perhaps it's an exaggeration to say that my search for the green leafy space took me all the way to Europe, but not much of one. A more immediate explanation is that I was scared. All around me, things were changing; what had begun as a fringy taste for violence by a small group of extremists had blossomed into a full-fledged trend affecting every level of what we euphemistically called "the movement." No longer could one participate in an antiwar demonstration without considering the likelihood that someone in the crowd was there to incite a riot. No longer could we assume that no one would be armed.

There was another thing that contributed to my disillusionment as well; I had glimpsed the future and found it wanting. Were the people who had determined the path of the student antiwar movement through political machinations in Cleveland really the ones to whom I wanted to apply for a passport? I doubted it. But there was also a deeper, more philosophical, uneasiness gnawing away at my political resolve, and it had to do with who I was and how I wanted to live.

Let me put it this way: there is a relationship between uncertainty and mystery. The two are like an old married couple that can't live apart; when one leaves your life, so goes the other. The YSA had robbed me of uncertainty. And while I could live without that, mystery was a component of the human condition without which I didn't feel alive at all. When uncertainty returns it brings mystery with it, dragging it by the arm, trembling, reluctant, shy, badly shaken but still alive. And only when mystery returns do you realize that she was ever gone.

There was a flaw in my life, and it had to do with imagining that there was an ultimate Truth and that I knew what it was. For the other side of knowing is complacency, and complacency is a kind of death. The other side of knowing is the absence of mystery and what dawned on me now was how much I mourned its passing. How I missed its jagged edges and the constant undulations of its changing form. How I longed to dance with mystery, to take it in my arms, to lie with it, kiss its lips and feel the gentle fingers of mystery playing in my hair. Somehow I had let mystery allude me; it had left my house and I wanted to open a door for its return.

As the temper of the times changed, I began to feel that I was seriously out of step. And so I had decided to leave America in the summer 1970, even if just for a while. I had bought a one-way ticket and, with no steady income nor concrete plan, parked my backpack in the streets of Amsterdam. The city was beautiful. The canals were beautiful. The flirtatious blonde girls speaking their own indecipherable language were beautiful.

Beautiful too was the inside of Hashish Hall, the crowded club on Prince Hendrikkade Street where, I soon learned, many of my fellow expats gathered daily. It was named, of course, for the primary activity that took place there. Literally consisting of a long hallway lined with benches on both sides, you could simply saunter in, take a seat and wait for the chillum to be passed your way.

A chillum is a straight conical clay pipe with a glowing dab of green or brown hashish at its business end. Invented in India, it had been used by wandering Hindu monks since at least the 18th century. Since the mid-1960s, however, the culture of owning and smoking chillums had been spreading to Western Europe – and later America – where the instrument's production and embellishment had become a folk art.

The smoking end of the pipe is open, and that's where the skill comes in; the ability to cover it with your mouth (aided by a hand-held rag) completely enough to prevent any smoke from escaping. If you did it just right you could get one good hit concentrated enough to take care of you for the rest of the day. Not to worry, though; if your turn was a long time coming or you lacked the dexterity to successfully suck, by mid-morning there was usually enough ambient smoke in the room to just take a whiff and be carried away.

It was into this atmosphere that I landed with a thud at the end of the '60s. It was an exciting time to be there, among thousands of fellow "freaks" from around the world fleeing their various cultures into the international counterculture we shared. It very quickly became obvious, though, that for some the journey ended where the hashish began. Determined not to follow their example, I strapped on my pack, spent a few nights in a local youth hostel and set off for other parts.

Yet despite my best intentions, it was hard to break free. An American expat with whom I'd become friendly gave me a going-away present as I climbed aboard a train bound for West Berlin. "For those cold German nights," he said, pressing a small clump of hashish into my palm. I thanked him, stuck it inside my boot where I believed it would be safe, and thought of it no more.

Until the train stopped at an East German border point just short of entering the city's Western sector. "*Ausweiss bitte!*" the guard said as he and his two cohorts made their way slowly down the aisle checking passports. At the seat directly in front of mine, occupied by a well-groomed young man, the trio stopped. "*Ausweiss bitte*," one of them said, and then, after inspecting the document, went on in broken English: "Please stand up."

As I watched in rising panic, they started patting him down, first running their hands loosely over his clothes, then removing his jacket and going through its pockets. Finally, as I looked on in horror, they ordered him to take off his shoes and ran their fingers along the inside edges. Suddenly the hashish in my boot felt like a burning ember. Should I make a move to throw it out the window and risk drawing attention to myself, or just utter a silent prayer? Christ, I thought, I'm trapped.

To fully appreciate the situation, a little historic perspective is required. This was the height of the Cold War, with the Soviet Union still intact and East Germany firmly under the dictatorial control of the Communists, separated from the West by a cold, impenetrable and fully functional Berlin Wall. It would be nearly two decades before the hated wall was dismantled and the city and country reunified. In 1970, though, East Germany was still staunchly "protecting" its citizens from "decadent" Western influences. It did that by maintaining rigid control over their interaction with foreigners and their access to anything coming from outside, be they products or ideas. Though the country's official position was that, unlike the West, it *had* no drug problem, we had all heard stories of people disappearing there for that and far lesser crimes. And because the U.S. maintained no diplomatic relations with East Germany, an American finding himself in such a predicament could hardly expect any help. In a word, I was *more* than potentially fucked.

Before I could formulate a plan, the man in front was putting on his jacket and the guards proceeding towards me. If a clean-cut guy like that got searched, I thought in dismay, what chance was there for a long-haired scruffian like me? Pursing my lips and blinking fast, I tried to think of a prayer, but came up blank. And then the miracle happened. The guards made a perfunctory check of my passport and passed right on by. Holy Mother of God, I thought, I'm safe. To this day, I have no idea why. When the train finally stopped in West Berlin I hopped off it and, for the first time in my life, felt like kissing the damp muddy ground. Then I met my first *real* Nazi.

10.

Nazis

Perhaps that's a bit harsh; he was a Nazi only if you consider the condition genetic like blond hair. As is true of most people currently alive, my idea of Nazis comes primarily from Hollywood. Thus, while it is entirely possible that a real one would have stormed onto a train screaming "*achtung, achtung,*" the only way I knew that was from seeing it in the movies. I bring this up because the true character of Nazism was to become a major theme of my stay in West Berlin.

Before going any further, I should give you a little family history: my Uncle Joe's favorite slogan was "scratch a *goy,* you got a *fascist.*" Perhaps that's because he was a survivor of Auschwitz. One of my earliest memories, in fact, was the bottomless pit I felt in my stomach after seeing the six-digit number tattooed on the forearm of his wife, Aunt Claire, my mother's younger sister.

As young Jews growing up in Germany of the 1930s, the sisters very early developed the paranoia that comes of not knowing whether any particular night would be their last. Born in a town called Chemnitz in what later became East Germany (the communists renamed it Karl Marx Stadt during their reign), Mom was still a child when Hitler came to power. Once, she told me, she was laughing on a balcony of the family's apartment as a procession of soldiers marched by. The laughter ended abruptly, however, when an SS officer pounded on the door demanding to take her away. "My mother screamed and begged him not to," she recalled. "She said, 'I will punish her more than you ever could,' and beat me bloody on the spot to prove that she would. Finally, he went away satisfied, and everyone cried."

One day Mom came home from college to an empty house. Years later, her sister told her what had happened: the Gestapo came for everyone in the middle of the night. Eventually taken to Auschwitz, most of the family died in the infamous gas chambers. Aunt Claire survived, got married, and immigrated to Philadelphia where she and her husband owned a woman's clothing boutique for many decades. And Mom managed to make it to Shanghai, China, where she spent the next 10 years living in a refugee camp under the tight control of the Japanese occupiers.

It was there, sometime before Pearl Harbor, that my father – a merchant seaman from Montana with several Methodist ministers in his family – met her during a random shore leave. Later his family sponsored her emigration to the United States where they married and, in 1949, played a central role in my own unceremonious entrance upon the earthly stage. Bottom line: whoever coined the term "baby boomer" to describe the post-war surge in stork deliveries was definitely talking about *me*.

. . .

I thought about all that as I wandered the streets of West Berlin, surprised at the number of bombed-out buildings still half-standing twenty-five years after the war. Had I been able to look into the future, I might also have thought about a chance meeting I would have thirteen years later with one of my literary heroes, Herman Wouk, who'd written, among many other things, *War and Remembrance* and *Winds of War*. Those two books, in particular, tell the story of World War II and its aftermath, including the ambivalence and struggle of young people born after the war – often of mixed parentage – regarding their Jewish vs. American identities.

Nazis and Nudists

I was in the middle of reading them in 1983 when – as part of the research for a newspaper feature on the rise of Orthodox Judaism in Palm Springs, California – I attended services at a small *schul* in that town and, praise God, there he was! I will never forget the brief conversation we had in which I told him my family's story. "I'm very glad to meet you," the great man said, shaking my hand. "You are *exactly* who I wrote those books *for.*" He even gave me a private number to call for personal lessons on Judaism which, to my eternal regret, I never called.

Perhaps that was due, in part, to the sense of resolution I'd achieved in Berlin with Klaus Rick, an emotional artist and actual son of an actual Nazi. I didn't know that right away, of course; if I had, we might never have become friends. As it happened, we met in a student cafeteria where both of us were scrimping for cheap meals. Recognizing each other by our shared countercultural badge – the dire absence of even the simple vestiges of a basic haircut – we immediately struck up a conversation. And by evening, in true hippie fashion, I was ensconced in a sleeping bag on the floor of the small flat he shared with his wife, a pretty young hausfrau named Bridgette. My residency there was to last nearly six months.

Klaus and I kicked off our relationship in a completely predictable way: by finishing off the clump of illicit hashish that had almost gotten me arrested. In the months that followed, we tended to rely more on a cultural mainstay and much cheaper entity for our nightly entertainments, namely beer. Often we'd go trawling for it in the pubs and end up drinking way too much. "Klaus," I'd say, slapping him affectionately on the back. "Tell me about your childhood. What was it like growing up as a kraut?"

"OK then," he'd say, laughing, "My father was a hunter. A big Bavarian with a beer belly and huge bulging muscles."

I could see it all. Klaus' father staggering home after a long day in the woods, sitting by the fireplace with his mug of beer, telling stories.

Klaus sitting on his knee bug-eyed, mama in the kitchen. One night, after an especially vigorous drinking bout, Klaus stayed up late drawing a portrait of his dad. When it was finished he held it up for me to see, smiling proudly like a child displaying his completed homework. "This is what he looked like," Klaus said with tears in his eyes. "He died of a heart attack when I was 10. This is the closest I've ever come. I believe I've got him at last." He pulled a handkerchief from his pocket and dabbed his eyes.

"You really loved your father, didn't you?" I said, laying a hand on my friend's shoulder.

"Very much," Klaus said, folding the handkerchief and smiling through water-clogged eyes. "I remember when he would come home late. Always on nights the party met. How we used to worry; how we hugged him when he arrived."

"Party?" I inquired.

"Yes, the Nazi Party," Klaus said. "Dad was an old radical, you know."

Actually I hadn't. And to make matters worse, my friend had just forced me into an uncomfortable realization: that even Nazis had children who loved them.

"My dad used to come home late too," I told him uneasily. "On nights that he worked overtime. Mom would get nervous at 10 minutes after five and by five-thirty she'd be hysterical."

Once she'd told me why. Jews in Hitler's Germany, she said, were never far from that midnight knock on the door and every time someone was late they'd assume the worst which, of course, eventually happened. Though Mom was a child, the fear stayed with her for life.

I explained all this to Klaus as he listened with widening eyes. When I'd finished he made an odd face, as if tasting something sour while feeling amused at his own pain.

"I've never met a Jew before," my friend quietly confessed.

"You're the first."

"I guess we're pretty much like anybody else," I countered nervously.

Klaus paused before replying. "I guess mothers are the same everywhere," he sighed finally. "How about a toast to mothers?"

To some extent fathers are too. Most of them love their families and do what they think is right. But even when what they do is evil, I realized, it is possible for people to live in more than one dimension. The man who murders by night can still play baseball with his kids by day. It was an insight into the complexities of human existence that was to serve me well in the years to come, especially in the pursuit of what would ultimately become my chosen profession, the practice of journalism.

"A toast to mothers sounds perfect," I said. Klaus and I linked arms, kicked open the door and, laughing, dove out into the brightly-colored night. Already, though, I was thinking of my next stop, a place where Nazis would be vastly outnumbered by nudists.

David Haldane

11.

Nudists

What followed can only be described as a 13-year-old boy's vision of paradise: a remote Greek island populated by naked women with lots of gnarly substances to drink and imbibe.

I decided to go to Mykonos, frankly, because I'd begun fancying myself a writer and thought there might be a novel in it. Also because, in the exuberance of youth, it seemed like the next logical place to continue my search for the ultimate spiritual and physical tranquility. Getting there, on the other hand, proved significantly more complicated than fantasizing about it. The trip took two weeks - first south from Berlin to Munich, followed by a long trek down through what was then Yugoslavia with a crazy Afghani who picked me up by the side of the road and kept driving up exit ramps. We slept by his Volkswagen where, every morning at six, he'd wake me up with the *briiinnngggg* of a tiny bell. I'd open my eyes and he'd be standing over me in baggy white pants that looked like pajamas. "Rise up my friend. We make go, no?" he'd say, his voice coming at me as if through 12 inches of solid brick wall.

We finally parted company in Athens where it was nothing but hot and I ended up sleeping on the cement floor of a youth hostel overflowing with American hippies. But islands were in my heart, and so I caught the ferry over to Mykonos. It was overwhelmingly white. White cobblestone streets, white houses and, everywhere, little white churches. Wandering idly through the streets of Chora, then just a sleepy little Greek village, I browsed through the array of leather sandals and belts hanging for sale in the little white shops.

"Eh, you look at belts?" a smiling shopkeeper asked in broken English. He was a muscular dark-haired man with black eyes. "If you wanna belt, I make you a good one." Then, after studying me up and down, "Eh, you new here? You gotta place to stay?"

I pleaded guilty to the first and responded negatively to the second. "Come with me then," he said, "to the other sidda the island. I'm Theo." He stuck out his hand.

Governments have their secrets, I thought as we marched out of town toward his car. Men have their dreams, lakes their bottoms and islands their other sides. I was off to see the other side of this one. But dirt roads have their bumps as well. "Ouch!" I cursed, bouncing in the back of his pickup like a coffee bean in a half-full can.

"Is all right!" Theo yelled out the window, barely audible in the din. "We be there soon."

And all around me, over me, through me, Greece was unfolding. Blue, brown, white, green Greece. Mile after mile of stone fences, and sheep, and stooped old ladies wearing black veils shuffling along dusty roads, with the wind whistling through my hair and the bluest water I'd ever seen. There was music bouncing down the road ahead of us, and we couldn't quite catch it, but we were trying, we were trying.

"One mile more," Theo yelled out the window, holding up a single finger. One more mile with the music still in front, the fields still water colored and the sky still big enough to suck one in. At last we arrived at *Platos Gialos,* the most developed and accessible of the white-sand beaches at the island's south end. Theo scrambled out of the cab like a drunkard retrieving his last bottle. "Now we walk," he said, taking off along the beach, drawn forward by some invisible energy bigger than both of us as I trotted behind.

"Is this it, Theo?" I asked, almost out of breath, "How much further?"

"This is first beach," he informed me. "We go to third beach. Very good beach."

There were tourists everywhere: muscular brown men with glistening European skin, slim topless bikinied ladies on beach towels strewn with tubes of suntan lotion and the sun streaming down on us like God's own body heat. As we reached the far end of the beach, the crowd thinned and suddenly we were climbing up a narrow dusty trail to the top of a hill. As far as I could see, the land was crisscrossed by crude stone fences.

"This way," said Theo, following one of the steep stone embankments. "These are the fields of the shepherds. The fences divide them." Below us, stretching for miles, was the blue sea. Looking back we could see the beach, tiny now, inhabited by moving specks like the balls in a distant arcade game. The land was dry and parched and rocky, and the wind hit our faces like blasts from a furnace.

In Greek mythology, Mykonos was named after its first ruler, Mykons, the grandson of Apollo, the mythological god of music, and a local hero. The island is also said to have been the site of a great battle between Apollo's father, Zeus, and an army of giants called Titans who were finally defeated here. Local lore even has it that the large rocks all over Mykonos are the giants' petrified testicles, hence the slang term "stones" used almost universally to describe those often over-glorified sets of reproductive organs.

Navigating among the rocks, we frequently passed little abandoned stone shelters. Occasionally we'd stop at one, get out of the sun, share a drink from Theo's canteen, perhaps a cigarette and some talk before moving on. Then suddenly the land levelled off and the sea dropped away; we were like insects caught in a hurricane of brown earth and blue sky.

Eventually we reached *Paradise Beach*, the second strand much less populated than the first. Without stopping we crossed it and continued our trek along the ridge overlooking the sea. An hour later, thirsty and tired, we were standing on a rock grinning down at the third beach below. "This is it," Theo said quietly. "*Super Paradise*. This is home." Without another word, he peeled off his clothes, folded them into a bundle on his shoulder and began scrambling down among the rocks like a naked spider.

    I slipped out of my clothes too and stood looking after him. It would be three months before I'd put them back on.

12.

Getting Off

It felt as if every bone in my body was broken. It was a pulsating kind of pain that surged and receded with each beat of the heart, filling muscles thick with blood then sapping it away until they sagged heavy, hollow and dry. Ted and the pill lady each took an arm and helped me up to my tent.

To be strictly accurate, it wasn't a tent at all but a crude lean-to, one of about a dozen constructed of driftwood on the sand housing a virtual village of people like me. The community consisted of perhaps 20 hippies – a core whose number waxed and waned – comprising a sort of countercultural United Nations. The main thing its delegates had in common was an alienation from the various countries that once had provided them succor. Now they all lay in the sun of *Super Paradise* beach baking to a golden hue – or, in my case, lobster red – frequently plunging into the ocean to bathe and making love whenever they pleased. When we got hungry, one of the women would cook something over a campfire or we'd walk to the only restaurant on the beach and beg for food. And when we needed a buzz, well, that could usually be achieved with, as the Beatles put it, a little help from our friends.

My favorite friend was the young English woman we called the "pill lady" who made daily rounds of our makeshift campsite carrying a large candy jar full of colorful little yellow pills. The story was that she had made a big score in the London drug market, stuffed three thousand bucks worth of goods into that jar and was dealing her way around the world, but for us everything was free. "What is it today?" I asked one morning towards the end of summer. "Oh," she said, "That's speed. It'll make you feel good." As it happened, that's exactly how I wanted to feel and so took two. Then jumped into the crystalline blue waters of the Aegean for a swim.

By then we had fallen into a daily routine on the beach. It usually began around 7 a.m. when Ted – a wannabe artist from New York whose perfect golden body looked like that of an *actual* Greek god – would shake me awake in my sleeping bag in time to watch the first boatload of tourists arrive. One morning the pill lady came shuffling up through the sand carrying a huge steaming pot. "Goat's stew for breakfast," she announced cheerily. "With something special for dessert."

We could, of course, imagine the hallucinogenic wonders her dessert had in store. At 19, she was an imposing figure with big solid breasts, sturdy shoulders and short curly brown hair reminiscent of Little Orphan Annie's. She was also something of a mother figure who, in addition to being an excellent supplier of dope, good cook and wonderful up lifter of spirits, had a quick wit that dripped of irony, self-mockery and sarcasm. The first time I saw her she was walking along the shoreline lugging a portable typewriter.

"What are you doing with that?" I asked.

"Looking for a place to write," she said. "Know of any?"

"What are you writing?" I plunged on, perhaps thinking of my own unrealized literary pretensions.

"There's a novel here somewhere," she said without skipping a beat, "but I can't seem to find it. Been searching for days; if you happen to stumble on it, please let me know."

Years later I would fantasize about the unconsummated erotic potential of my daily encounters with this big woman who went looking for novels in the buff. In addition to her many other services, she seemed to be sexually available to just about any male on the island who wanted her. For some inexplicable reason, I never thought much about it, though, now that I *am* thinking about it, it's entirely possible – perhaps even *likely* – that she serviced me in that way at least once or twice. In any case, I've often wondered what became of the English woman with the jar full of pills and the novel lost in sand.

• • •

Once Ted and I accepted the offer of a Greek boatman to ferry us down the coast in the middle of a perfectly bottomless afternoon. The man steered his craft with an expert hand, catching spray in his mouth as he laughed – strong, manly, confident – and I looked out over the sea through happy eyes thinking that there are certain moments when time acts like a rubber band; flexible, stretchable and capable of overlapping. Sometimes we aren't aware of the overlap until years later when the moment is re-experienced and we perceive the cycle, realize that the new moment is just like the old; that, in effect, they are one and the same, kind of an eternal moment that, with luck, we can tap into throughout our lives. Perhaps, it even occurred to me, this was the ultimate object of my restless search: the permanent moment transcending time.

In fact, it was in just such a moment – though fleeting – that Ted and I found ourselves on that voyage, laughing in the wind and spray with a kind of masculine joy surging through us like blood through the veins of wild animals. Perhaps it was a desire to relive that moment that, days later, propelled me into the ocean fortified by those little yellow pills.

To be honest, I felt like a god. As I slid, stroke by stroke, out to sea I knew that I could do anything. It was as if I had somehow slipped the bounds of biology and physics to perform feats heretofore available only in dreams. Pulled along by a strong current of euphoria, I just kept on swimming. And swimming. And then swimming some more. By the time I turned around, six hours had passed and I could barely see land. So I spent another six hours swimming back the same way I'd come.

When I finally – and, I might add, *miraculously* – got washed back ashore, my two best friends, by then quite worried, dragged me out of the water and tucked me into a sleeping bag. It was only upon regaining consciousness several days later that I felt intense pangs of hunger amidst every muscle afire.

Let me at least say this: It was the last time I ever took those little yellow pills. Otherwise I might never have escaped this hellish nirvana to continue my search. That escape began the morning, not too long after almost drowning, that I inadvertently interrupted a blowjob. I had gone to visit Ted and the pill lady who, not surprisingly, had moved into the shelter next to mine, which I often visited unannounced. "Hello" she said, looking up from her task long enough to smile slyly as she brushed Ted's ample, and quite erect, organ gently against her cheek. "To what do we owe this pleasure?"

"I'm leaving," I announced. "It's time for me to go."

"Why would you do a crazy thing like that?" the pill lady wanted to know.

It was a question I'd been asking myself, so far without a satisfactory answer. "It's hard to explain," I tried to explain. "Maybe because it's so damed comfortable. Maybe because it's too soon to let myself be lulled. Maybe because I think there's more."

"Oh David," she said dreamily, "no one ever really leaves here, you know that."

In my case that came very close to being true. Perhaps, I later came to believe, it even *was* true. Suffice it to say that there was something of a lag between the announcement of my departure and its actual occurrence. The process began two weeks later when I met an American expat named Bob who said he had an apartment in Paris and a BMW motorcycle parked in an Athens garage. If we could make it that far, he assured me, he would give me a ride up the Italian coast to France from where I could go anywhere I wanted.

Our plan was to walk back to the port at Chora on the other side of the island, catch a boat to the mainland and be on our way. But that proved to be easier said than done; like a woman wearing intoxicating perfume, the island had mystical ways of enforcing its invisible hold on anyone who stayed long enough to take off his clothes. Some might even say that it was a form of entrapment, a sort of magical chain that couldn't be seen nor felt, yet boasted links strong enough to imprison anyone presuming to resist.

Whatever the reason, it took us three attempts to even make it onto the gangplank. The first time we took off in broad daylight with the full knowledge and support of our fellow inmates who clapped us on the back, offered hugs and cheerfully bid us good luck and adieu. We made it as far as the second beach – perhaps a small step down from *Super Paradise,* but *Paradise* nonetheless – where still other friends offered to buy us farewell drinks in a bar familiar to us all. "Let's do this right," they insisted, "a last party, a final farewell."

The next morning, hung over with the boat from Chora long gone, we woke up in strange sleeping bags provided by some generous soul. "Fuck it," Bob said, "let's give it another week." And so we did.

The second attempt was somewhat more successful; we got as far as the line waiting to board the boat on the dock. Tickets in hand, we tarried nervously as a man wearing a skipper's cap worked his way down the line. When he was three passengers ahead of us, Bob looked at me and I looked right back. "I can't do this," he said.

"Neither can I."

It took us exactly five seconds to tear up our tickets, a mere fraction of that to hop out of line and about half an hour to hitch back to *Platos Gialos.*

Ah, but it was the third try that finally stuck, or perhaps I should say *unstuck*. This time we arose at 3 a.m. and, before anyone even knew we were gone, had trudged surreptitiously with our backpacks over the dusty hills to the village. It was a magnificent morning in Greece with endless miles of ocean illuminated by the sunrise; a great palette of colors stretching out like a carpet before us. Soon we were sitting on the dock, waiting for the 8 a.m. boat.

"Hey man, what were you doing in Greece anyway?" Bob asked through a yawn.

A cascade of images flashed through my mind, finally settling on the figure of the pill lady trudging through the sand with her portable typewriter.

"Looking for a novel," I said.

"Oh yeah? Ever find it?"

I paused, carefully considering my reply. "Naw," I said. "It's lost in the sand on the other side of the island."

"Too bad," Bob said.

I hesitated a moment longer. "It'll turn up one of these days," I said. "Some Greek fisherman will stub his toe on it pulling in his nets and take it home to his children and all the neighbors will talk about it for months, and they'll have lots of visitors."

The bottomless moan of a bone-chilling foghorn interrupted our conversation. The boat had arrived. I was on my way back to a place that I would hardly recognize.

13.

Jerusalem

Back in America, the earth – or at least the part of it with which I was most familiar – had shifted in my absence. Ever since its inception, the counterculture had been informally divided into two major factions: the *innies* represented by the hippies, and the *outies* represented by the various brands of politicos including those advocating violent revolution. The difference between the two had to do with philosophy and lifestyle; while *innies* believed that changes in society began with changes within its individual members, *outies* argued that it was society's *institutions* that had to be changed, sometimes by any means necessary.

By the time I returned to the country of my birth, it was clear that the influence of the *outie* faction – the hard politics of radicalism – had already peaked and, except for a few stragglers like those about to kidnap Patty Hearst, was on the wane. The influence of the *innies* – the softer "touchy-feely" kind of activism – on the other hand, was still going strong.

In effect, the prevailing message of the counterculture had evolved. In the early years it had gone something like this: the world is corrupt, but we can change it. Now there was a new message: the world is corrupt, but we can live in it. How? By creating our own alternate world to thrive within the old one, a sort of parallel universe in which we could hide in plain sight. The expectation: that ultimately our world would survive and the other one perish.

That sounded just fine to me. And so I made my way to what seemed like the burgeoning capitol of that parallel universe: Berkeley, California.

The place was a cauldron of delicious subversion. I parked myself in a boarding house just off Telegraph Avenue where the entire circus was on parade. Then set out for the offices of the *Berkeley BARB*. In truth, I'd never been to a real newsroom before. But someone had said that the paper needed layout artists, and I'd done a little of that for the college paper back at Goddard. So I threw some samples into a backpack and set off across town.

The *BARB* didn't look like much by 1973. The front of the place lay plastered under hundreds of dried posters slapped atop each other like layers of ageing tree bark chronicling the history of the time. A pair of them caught my eye: one bore the familiar visage of Cuban revolutionary Che Guevara, then still venerated by many in Berkeley, set off by the slogan *Venceromos* – "We Shall Triumph!" Half covering it, though, was a newer poster, this one adorned by the face of a plump dark-skinned young boy and the words "Who is Maraj-Ji?" I sucked in my breath and opened the door.

Max Scherr was still editor in those days, and the inside of the place looked pretty much like the outside. The old man occupied a back corner of the room, facing the wall at a desk piled high with books, papers, unopened letters and yellowed issues of the *BARB*. "Whadaya want?" he said without turning around. He seemed to be scribbling rapidly on the back of an envelope atop all that crud.

"Hi, uh, I'm David Haldane. I was wondering whether you need any help."

Only then did he look over his shoulder, staring at me thoughtfully through piercing brown eyes. They peaked out from behind an enormous grey-black beard topped by long scraggly hair of the same color. He wore a cap, riding on his sea of hair like a little boat about to capsize. Though seemingly calm, he had the look of a man perfectly capable of biting off your nose. Max swiveled around in his chair, leaned back and studied me coldly with fingers laced tightly behind his head. "And just how do you think you can help, young man?" he asked.

"I can lay out a page," I said, handing him a sample. As it happened, some of the pieces I'd laid out also bore my byline. Without a word, he began scanning them. "I see that you also can write," Max said suddenly. "Tell you what – I've got an assignment for you." And just like that, my career in journalism began.

The story he had in mind was about a man named Pat McSorely, though neither of us yet knew that name. In fact, most people – if they knew him at all – referred to him simply as the blind beggar of Berkeley, the city's oldest and most persistent panhandler in a town that celebrated that pursuit. At 73, McSorely was a familiar figure on Telegraph Avenue where he spent most days clutching a red-tipped cane in one hand and rattling a tin cup in the other. He'd been at it so long that he'd become a local fixture whose tale, Max felt, should finally be told. And so he sent me out to get it.

"I usually work six or seven hours a day," the old man told me over tacos at La Fiesta, a popular Mexican restaurant in town. "If I'm lucky I can make $1.60; on a really good day maybe twice that. Sometimes things get good and sometimes they slack up, you never can tell."

Then he told me a story almost too perfect to believe. Born in nearby Vallejo, McSorely said, he was one of eleven children of a poor tailor who died when he and he and his siblings were young. But cruel fate intervened even further when a clump of exploding gun powder blinded young Pat in one eye and, a short time later, a careless archer shot out the other. McSorley said he attended a school for the blind for a time but got kicked out for bad behavior. Then he tried making baskets and, failing in that, finally took to the streets.

For two hours he regaled me with stories of his Berkeley life. Some of them were incredible, like the one about the plainclothes policewoman who invited him to dinner, then handed him the bill. Or the priest who had him arrested. "I don't mind being blind," McSorely concluded, "I'm used to it. I've met thousands of people, most of them good. But, boy, some of them are just damn crooks. Most dogs will treat you better than people, at least they're on the level. I love a good dog."

The story appeared a few days later under the title "Blind Man's Bluff." The morning it came out, I was having coffee at the Renaissance Cafe' when I noticed a complete stranger reading my piece. An unfamiliar, but also quite pleasant, sense of omnipotence and wellbeing swelled up in my bosom. Thus began a lifelong addiction to ink which, in Berkeley, was a gateway to mischief and magic.

For it wasn't just crusty posters proclaiming that God was a fat kid. A few weeks after my arrival, no less a luminary than Rennie Davis blew into town to announce that he too had come to that conclusion. This was big news in Berkeley; Davis had been a staunch antiwar activist, a defendant in the infamous Chicago 7 conspiracy trial following major disruptions at the 1968 Chicago Democratic National Convention, and someone columnist Nicholas von Hoffman had described as "the most stable, the calmest, the most enduring of that group of young people who set out to change America at the beginning of the 1960s." Now here he was, proclaiming that God was an overweight Indian teenager who would usher in the new millennium – a thousand years of "perfect peace" – at a gathering set for Houston in November. The initial reaction was predictable: people threw tomatoes in Zellarbach Auditorium.

After the hubbub subsided, however, Davis returned – this time more quietly – and offered an interview to the *Berkeley BARB*. "Haldane, I think this one's yours," the managing editor, James A. Schreiber, yelled across the newsroom for no particular reason, and off I went.

It was a rainy night and the first time I'd driven my ancient Honda

150 across the bay. Every car that passed made the rickety motorcycle shudder as if for the last time, producing an acute sensation of being on the verge of extinction. The Bay Bridge has a way of arching over the water like a crystalline reflection of moonbeam on windy nights. Wet pavement chomps at your tires, the greedy licks of a hungry troll just daring you to cross. Beyond bay water, the lights of the city swim in their own amalgam of soup; rainwater, night air, moonlight, city lights – a regular tango of the elements swaying slightly back and forth, jiggling together, then separately; rainwater on city light, moonlight on night air, like buttered lobster for an artist's eye.

I found Davis cross-legged and barefoot in the middle of a carpet in the otherwise empty living room of a large Victorian house in San Francisco's Fillmore district. Despite the darkness outside, he gave the uncanny impression of being bathed in light. Cloaked in white, he sat with his eyes closed, blissfully smiling as a pretty blonde-haired woman gave him a sensuous backrub. "Hello David," he said without opening an eye. "Welcome to Divine Light Mission." Without further ado, he began describing the process that had transformed him from a run-of-the-mill Marxist into a gushing Marxist-Guruist.

It was quite simple, really; he'd been on a flight to Paris when two fellow passengers convinced him that their guru was God. "I spent most of that trip with guys whose politics were very much like my own," Rennie explained. "They weren't flipped out at all. And their main message was that any analysis for interpreting world events would become less and less useful in explaining what will be coming down in the very near future. To understand that, you must understand the central event of our time, the presence on earth of Guru Maharaj Ji."

What, exactly, did that presence portend, I asked. Well, Davis said, along with the much-advertised perfect peace, the guru would usher in a new society based on service not status. "It won't matter what role you play," Davis said. "Whether you're the mayor or wash clothes, the only function of service will be to realize knowledge."

It sounded like washed-over socialism. "Honestly," I said, "that just seems weird."

"Actually," Davis said, exhibiting a bit of the smoothness for which he was famous, "it struck me the same way at first. What was the most bizarre was hearing people say that they really believed this guru was God. For me that immediately triggered, 'Oh this is a religion' -- something I've always been really clear about not spending a whole lot of energy on."

"So what happened?" I asked.

"I don't exactly know," he said as amiably as an old friend. "I've always been kind of reflective, kind of in touch with things and going through pretty much what everybody else was going through. I was getting more into spirituality and doing some yoga. When Lyndon Johnson died, I felt like we were entering a new era; I kept telling everyone it's going to be a dark age and people have to overcome their fear of death. I was thinking that it might be nice to spend some time just reflecting, meditating, and I thought, well, if I'm going to meditate I should have a meditation technique. Two weeks later I was with Guru Maharaj Ji."

"But a 15-year-old fat kid from India?" I snickered. "I'm sorry, I just don't get it."

He looked at me with benign patience, as if speaking to a child. "You know," he finally said, "it's as if I had a box in my hand and I told you, 'Take a look through the hole in this box and you'll see God.' And you say, 'Oh man, you must have fallen out of a banana tree, you're crazy.' And I say, 'No, listen, you take a look in here and I'm telling you, you'll see God.' So you say you don't believe in God. And I say, 'I'm not asking you to believe, man, just take a look and tell me what you see.' Essentially that's what Maharaj Ji is saying only it's not a box, it's your own human body. You experience the knowledge that he reveals in the classic way that all the scriptures talk about God, as a light and a primordial vibration. Guru Maharaj Ji has a gift that can transform the human race; what we're talking about here is the greatest change in the history of human civilization."

• • •

The most obvious change, of course, was his own. I thought about that early the next morning as I strolled down Telegraph Avenue. The sun was barely up and as I shuffled along the deserted sidewalk, I stuffed my hands into my pockets to keep them warm and let my mind wander over the things minds tend to wander over on such barely mornings.

The color blue, for instance. Blue made you feel peaceful, calmed you down and cosmically connected you. But on mornings like this, blue had a frightening quality. On mornings like this, blue meant lost and it overwhelmed me, made me feel invisible and small. On mornings like this I felt an unutterable loneliness and unless I fought it, unless I screeched, hollered and flayed my arms about, it descended on me like a falling sky flinging me into a dark abyss from which I could emerge only in time.

As I walked down Telegraph Avenue, I kept my hands in my pockets and my eyes to the ground. Everywhere lay bits of broken glass and debris. In an hour the street would be waking up and on the glass would sit skinny longhaired young men with their hands out. Tourists would snap their pictures and hand them quarters. By afternoon the dirty-faced young men would be holding slender bottles of wine with which they would wash down varicolored pills. And by evening the wine bottles would have become broken bits of glass again.

In the coffee shops, intense-looking men with beards would soon be ordering their breakfasts and unfolding newspapers. And as the morning progressed, other intense-looking men with beards would join them, lay books on the table, offer smokes and begin passionate discussions that would last all day. By evening the smoke of their pipes and cigarettes would fill the coffee shops, making them impossible to enter without coughing.

As I walked down Telegraph Avenue, I kept my hands in my pockets and my eyes to the ground, but a bit of red stopped me. It was the poster I had seen before, the picture of the fat kid with dark skin under the slogan "Who is Guru Maharaj Ji?"

An old man with a face like pinched marshmallow was leaning against the poster looking at me and I couldn't resist an impulse to talk. "Who do *you* think he is?" I asked, nodding casually toward the wall. His eyes followed the direction of mine and suddenly lit up. "I don't know," he said, "maybe the devil."

I tossed him a quarter and moved on.

Very soon now beautiful women pushing baby carts and wearing long flowing dresses with nothing underneath would be strolling up and down Telegraph smiling at shirtless young men in straw hats. Everywhere one would feel the agreement men and women make before birth, the silent knowledge of eternity expressed in their secret erotic smiles. And even in the midst of all the blue, all the glass, all the smoke – even in the midst of torn posters and crusty saliva on old men's lips, one would feel a glimmer of hope, a twinge of anticipation.

Divine Light Mission's much-heralded Houston bash turned out to be a bust. By then I was beyond caring, though, because I had discovered something far more interesting: that I was living in the New Jerusalem.

I could hardly wait to begin exploring its streets.

14.

What the Voices Say

In the months that followed I met many street corner saviors.

A young Israeli psychic named Uri Geller, who years later would become one of Michael Jackson's closest friends and confidants, blew into town to demonstrate his prowess at telepathically bending spoons. "My powers do not come from me but originate somewhere out there," he insisted over lunch at the Claremont Hotel. "I am part of a plan, but not just me. We are moving very rapidly now toward something *big*."

Joanna Leary, Timothy's sweetheart, spoke to me on the couch of her mother's San Francisco apartment wearing a short skirt and no panties. Her subject: the upcoming Comet Kohoutek, which she and her old man were touting as the spiritual event of the century. "I communicate telepathically with beings of the Higher Intelligence," she patiently explained. "So could you if you just opened your mind; I can see transmissions coming down on your head."

And finally there was Zakatarious, the self-proclaimed reincarnated Minoan who had constructed an oft-displayed "golden calf" out of paper mache' that caused hippies to laugh and religionists to scream. His plan: to mount the thing on a trailer for a cross-country caravan ending on the White House lawn where President Richard Nixon himself would fall to his knees and confess his sins.

All of this I dutifully reported for the *BARB*. After a while, though, it wasn't enough, I wanted to go deeper. So gradually I changed my way of operating; instead of going in for the quick hit, I'd hang out with a subject just long enough to begin seeing the world through his or her eyes. Then I'd steal back to my digs on Channing Way for a first-person account. That's how I experienced reincarnation counseling, a method pioneered by Scientology ostensibly to jog one's memory regarding pre-birth identities. It's also how I participated in a séance and learned tantric yoga.

Preparing for tantra seemed somehow familiar. "I want you to go to a special place," the instructor said. "It is a place that exists only in your mind; a place of comfort and peace. It is where you go to escape, the place you call home."

I imagined myself at the top of a staircase descending deep into the darkness below. Though I had no idea what was down there, I knew I had to go. But the bottom wasn't a bare basement floor; instead it was a beautiful patch of cool grass on the bank of a river. I sat down and watched the water flowing by. And for a moment I was on another patch of grass, the one by the Vermont graveyard where my friends had found me laughing, the spot for which I'd been searching and still longed to find. It was as if the river, like time, was passing and yet stationery, flowing yet eternal and unchanging. Then the moment fled and I was just another reporter covering a story for the *Berkeley BARB*.

• • •

One day I walked into the newsroom and, following Rennie Davis' advice, peered into a box. It was my mailbox, and inside was a note from John Dosa, manager of a small local access cable company in nearby Newark inviting me to appear with Joanna Leary and others in a live Comet Kohoutek special airing that Friday night. Cable TV – especially *local access* – was still in its infancy then and, frankly, I hardly knew what it was. But it was the first time since Albany that I'd been asked to speak publically to anybody on anything, and so I said yes.

David Haldane

On the day of the broadcast, Dosa picked me up in Berkeley and drove me to the makeshift studio in a small room of his house. It was about the size of a playpen; two couches pushed together with a coffee table in front. Behind the table, lurking atop a tripod on wheels, sat the dinkiest video camera I'd ever seen.

It was 10 minutes to air time; Joanna had not yet arrived.

An heiress to the Harcourt-Smith publishing fortune, she had been raised in European luxury before giving it all up to become an American hippie. Then, at the tender age of 26, she met and fell in love with Timothy Leary, the 52-year-old acid guru himself, with whom she'd spent some time on the lamb in Europe and Afghanistan. By 1973, the couple was back in California; he in prison on a drug charge from an old bust in Laguna Beach, she his eyes and ears on the outside and tireless lobbyist for his release.

At the moment, though, they were loudly promoting the imminent appearance of Comet Kohoutek. Named after a Czech astronomer, the astronomical phenomenon was expected to create a spectacular aerial display to which various elements of the counterculture were assigning large amounts of spiritual significance.

On hand to discuss it tonight, in addition to myself, were two alleged experts: an incredibly fat psychic with clairvoyant brown eyes, short curly black hair and the loud bubbling voice of a matron, and a gaunt astronomer from a nearby observatory wearing a brown business suit. While the orbs of her bottom flowed over the edges of the couch like huge globs of butter, he sat meekly upright with hands on his knees and a briefcase tucked pertly under his seat. Frankly, he looked like he was expecting someone to rush out of the shadows at any moment and make him produce evidence.

One minute to air time Leary still hadn't shown, but Dosa didn't seem to notice. "All right," he said, glancing about the room. "Is everybody ready?"

"On with the show!" the psychic chortled.

The host adjusted a microphone at his throat, glanced at the clock and flipped on a switch. "Hi folks," he said, leaning back in his chair glancing casually into the camera. "Welcome to our Comet Kohoutek special. We have several guests here tonight to speak about the comet and what it means. And Joanna Leary should be arriving shortly with lots to say, I'm sure."

He introduced the guests one by one, saving me for last.

"Tell us, David," Dosa said, "how did you get interested in the comet?"

I was on. I stared into the camera. "Well, you know, everyone was talking about it and, you know, I just thought it would be interesting and, well, I started talking to people about it and they talked to me and, well, one thing led to another. You know?"

Suddenly there was a rustling as Joanna Leary waltzed in followed by five young men. Wearing white hot pants with a red sash, she looked dazzling. There were a few moments of chaos as the seating arrangements were made. In the midst of the confusion, someone placed an enormous bottle of champagne on the table along with eight or nine glasses. "Well," Dosa said, "you made it."

A small monitor on the floor was saturated with Joanna, only Joanna. The lens of the camera drank her in, sucking it out of her, only her, only Joanna Leary. "We got lost in a fog," Joanna said, looking slightly stoned. By now the cameraman had begun a long pan of her sitting figure. Beginning with the ankles, he moved slowly upward, pausing at her knees, her thighs, her crotch, and finally her breasts. As soon as the first pan was completed, he returned to her ankles for a second look.

"Tell me," Dosa said, "are you actually married to Timothy Leary?"

"Spiritually yes," she said. "I carry his name because we are spiritual spouses."

Somebody shoved a glass of champagne into my hand and I took a sip. "But the important thing tonight is Comet Kohoutek," Joanna said, and from that moment on she was in complete control. "The planet's a womb," she said, "and we've been seeded." The monitor on the floor was filled with a close-up of Joanna Leary's crotch.

For a long time I sat staring at it guzzling champagne. Twice the camera panned the whole scene, startling me with the sight of myself on the monitor. It was almost as if I were watching from my living room, unaware that I was actually in the studio.

Finally, as much to break the monotony as anything else, I decided to get into the game. "Listen Joanna," I said, surprised at the fuzziness of my own voice, "tell them about the Higher Intelligence."

Someone refilled my glass. The astrologist laughed. John Dosa looked bleary eyed. The astronomer sat silent. And Joanna Leary took the cue. "Well," she said, "what I'm getting from them right now is that things are about to start happening."

The five people she'd brought with her all nodded in agreement as one. Suddenly the phone, silent until now, startled us all with a ring. "Hello," said Dosa, picking up a receiver connected to a speaker for all to hear.

"John?" said a masculine voice, partially obscured by the sound clinking glasses in the background.

"Clement, that you? You watching the show?"

"You're on the air?" Clement asked.

The fat psychic laughed and took a sip of champagne as the host and his caller exchanged pleasantries. Finally Dosa hung up. "Sorry folks," he said, "this is my personal line too." Then he refocused on Joanna. "*What* things are about to happen?" Dosa wanted to know. "And what do you mean by Higher Intelligence?"

By then I had ceased staring at the monitor and was mesmerized by the wall above Joanna's head. It was trembling a little, dancing in the wind like I was seeing it through a wave of heat.

"I mean," Joanna said, "that I communicate with extraterrestrials who, at this time, are directing the course of events in the world through those, like me, with whom they communicate. Anyone can hear them; you just have to know how to listen. Timothy's writing a book about it. It's a manual on rocketry; we're leaving the earth."

I perked up. "But who will decide who gets to go?" I asked. "Won't that be kind of tricky?" I had emerged from the funk of the wall above Joanna's head just long enough to ask the question before returning my gaze there. I took another sip and waited for her reply.

"Of course it will be tricky," she said. "But it's not up to us; it's up to the Higher Intelligence. It's kind of like the time of Noah, you see. God decided who would be saved and who would remain. Same thing now. Those who are to be reborn are already receiving transmissions."

The phone rang again. "Hello," Dosa said. "This is Channel 12 and you're on the air."

"Excuse me?" a slurred male voice said, "on the where?"

"Air," Dosa said. "You have anything to say about Comet Kohoutek?"

"Commodore who?" said the man, clearly drunk.

Dosa hung up. "Strange things seem to be happening on the lines tonight," he said.

The astronomer's knees were touching. He cleared his throat.

"It's the effect of the comet," the psychic said. She went for her glass on the coffee table, but instead of retrieving it knocked it over. A puddle of champagne gathered like a lake on the floor. "Not only on the lines," she said. Then she resumed that infernal laughing, Lord that laughing, and all four walls seemed to waver a bit, uncertain of themselves, and for the first time I felt the pangs of fear.

"I want to know what messages everyone's receiving from the Higher Intelligence," Joanna announced. The camera zoomed in on her. "Let's go around the room and each of us tell what we're receiving."

She pointed to the big psychic, inviting her to go first. "Goodness gracious," the woman said, clearing her throat. "Well, all right, let me see what I can get. This may take some time." She folded her hands on her lap, closed her eyes and assumed the pose of a Buddha. An uneasy moment of silence ensued. Then another. Suddenly her lips began to move. "I see a space," she said. "A vast, *open* space. A *lonely* space. There's a glob of jelly floating in it and encased in the jelly – a new world! We are leaving the earth."

"Right on," muttered one of Joanna's cohorts.

"I'd like to hear from some other people," Joanna said. "John, what about you?"

Dosa closed his eyes as if in deep meditation. "Well, basically I get the same thing," he said. "Yeah, we're leaving the earth."

A guy named Peter, one of the boys Joanna had brought with her, went next. He was blond, fair-eyed and bearded - a California dream. He leaned back in his chair, closed his eyes and a blissful, faraway smile crept over his face. "I see beautiful gardens," he said. "It's a time of transition. We're moving out."

One by one Joanna pointed, and people talked about the voices they heard. Some spoke in riddles with their eyes closed, "transmitting" directly as if temporarily under the power of some extraterrestrial force. Others offered brief synopses of what they said the voices had told them. The images varied, but the messages were the same: we are in a period of transition, a new age is beginning and the future is bright, listen to the voices and do as they say.

At last only the astronomer and I hadn't spoken. "What about you, David?" Joanna said. "What are the transmissions telling you?"

I glanced about the room taking in the faces of all present, serene faces, faces looking at me with trust. For a moment I wavered, hesitant, uncertain of what to say. Then smiled straight ahead. The huge lens was glaring at me, bearing down like the barrel of a gun. I could see my reflection in the glass; a young man with long hair and dazed eyes like everybody else's. I wavered a moment longer, then made up my mind. "The voices say go," I said.

It hardly mattered what happened after that because the walls vibrated terribly like an airplane hitting wind. The thin astronomer's interrogation sounded like a hiss in the background and it was only later, upon reflection, that I remembered what was said.

"What about you," Joanna asked, "what do *you* hear?"

The astronomer sat as he had all night, hands folded neatly in his lap, leaning forward in his seat, knees touching, slightly trembling. He faced the barrel of the camera bravely with a hint of mockery like a man being executed.

"Why, I don't hear a thing," he said.

The vibrating sensation increased until I thought the walls would crumble and all of us be lost. That's when I knew that it was time to face the truth.

David Haldane

15.

Little Boxes

The truth was that I hadn't heard anything either. But in the days that followed I became increasingly cognizant of another truth: that a man hears what he wants to hear, it's just a matter of listening. Rennie Davis had been right about looking into the box. But there were a myriad of boxes in Berkeley and each had an eyepiece focused for a different eye. So you had to keep looking until you found one that appeared sharp to you, one in which you could read the fine print and see clearly the markings on its walls. And you had to listen too, for each box had a voice and each voice sang its own song.

    Lord how I'd looked. Lord how I'd listened. It had become a full-time occupation. I did nothing else but spend my days looking into boxes and describing what I saw. One day I looked into a box and saw my mentor, Max Scherr, sitting at the Mediterranean Café on a Friday afternoon. This was the archetypal smoke-filled room where the Berkeley heavies all hung out, but on this day I found Max alone, nursing a beer and looking sad. He motioned me to come over.

    A former bar owner himself, Max had started the *BARB* with his longtime companion, Jane Peters, in 1965. The scruffy "underground" paper quickly became the news and communications center for the militant Free Speech Movement then swelling on the Berkeley campus. That role was bolstered in 1969 when the *BARB*'s coverage made international headlines by sparking the infamous battle over People's Park, driving circulation to a startling 90,000 nationwide.

Now, however, things were changing; the political movement had ground its teeth almost flat and the protests were petering out. At about the same time, Max was encountering personal problems: Peters had left him and threatened to assume control.

It was 3 p.m. when I saw him. I had come in from the glare of the day looking for some coffee and a spot of peace after working all morning. Max was sitting at a table hunched over a newspaper and the mug of beer. "Hi Dave," he said without looking up, "working hard?"

"Always," I said, feeling uncomfortable. We sat in silence for a few moments sipping our drinks, Max reading the paper. "How are things with you?" I asked.

He folded the paper carefully on the table. "Hard times," my boss said. "I dunno, Dave, I just feel tired. The paper's dying and there's nothing I can do."

"What are you talking about?" I managed, nonplussed.

He turned his head to look around the room, but the effort proved almost too much; the head seemed heavier than the neck could support. It circled slowly like a top reaching the end of its spin, then toppled sidelong onto the table's surface. With great effort, he raised it again and faced me squarely.

"You weren't around," he said, "so you don't know. In the old days the *BARB* didn't just report the movement, it *created* it. We had good writers then, people who were willing to get out there and work. Hell, we *made* the movement; we weren't just a newspaper, we were *news*."

"And now?" I asked, almost afraid to hear his reply.

"Shit," said Max, waving his index and middle fingers weakly in the air, "nobody wants to do anything now, nothing's happening."

I thought about it for a second before responding. "Max, I don't think the *BARB* has changed as much as times have; things are different now, you can't get around that. The issues have changed, and it's a whole new game."

"Hell it is," said Max. "The issues never change. It's just that we don't always have the courage and perception to see them clearly. Nothing's changed but us; we're older and more tired."

He took another swig from his mug. "Now we're just like all the others," Max moaned. "I know what needs to be done, dammit, but I don't know anybody willing to do it. I think the seventies is an age of despair."

He swooned then, laid his head on the table and for an instant I thought he would cry. But he didn't; just picked up his head and kept sucking that beer.

In a way I understood how he felt. The times had indeed changed, and Max was definitely old school. Yet there was a kind of schizophrenia in his despair. While Max the ideologue still espoused countercultural political values, Max the businessman had ridden the crest of the change, in some ways even hastening it.

That was especially evident in the *BARB*'s classified advertising section where, as early as 1967, the customer base that had initially supported the paper – primarily head shops and the music industry – began giving way to an extensive, and increasingly prominent, collection of explicit personal sex ads. Eventually about a third of the paper displayed various forms of sexual advertising touting an array of earthly delights including X-rated films, pornographic bookstores, mail order novelties, both gay and straight erotic models, massage therapists and prostitutes of every ilk.

For a time the gratuitous nude photos spilling into the news section made the *BARB* one of the country's top-selling underground newspapers. In the end, though, it alienated the movement's more ideological components – especially feminists – and, perhaps even more significantly, began affecting coverage. So it wasn't surprising that, by 1974, I was writing explicit articles related to the "sexual revolution" regarded by many as a natural extension of the *inner* revolutionary direction the movement had taken.

A two-part series appearing under my byline in February of that year, for instance, featured a first-person exploration of the latest Bay Area rage – the Nude Encounter – during which generally male subjects paid for the "liberating" experience of engaging in private conversations with naked females. While the phenomenon broke no new ground for me personally, it seemed to have created quite a buzz among readers learning about it for the first time through advertisements in the *Berkeley BARB*. Naturally, the newspaper covered my expenses in personally researching the subject. But the distance from that to actual pornography was not very far.

In time, of course, this trend would prove to be the *BARB*'s undoing. In the early years of Scherr's "age of despair," however, it was potentially – and in some cases *actually* – a source of considerable profit. And so it happened that I got a call from a guy named Goff. "*Jack* Goff," he said, and we were off to the, um.....show.

16.

Sodom and Gomorrah

As a young idealist advocating the triumph of peace over war, it had never occurred to me that I would become a pornographer. Yet that's the direction in which Berkeley was stumbling. Euphoric, mystical visions of an ethereal future were taking on more earthly hues. Pornography, then transitioning from back-room-illegal to semi-respectable status, was increasingly seen as revolutionary art. And, inevitably, what had begun as the powerful and ecstatic trembling of a spiritual quest was daily being reduced to the quest for orgasmic spasms of a more physical kind. Which is how I ended up covering Jacquie Brody's strip show at the New Follies Theater of Burlesque.

Ostensibly, Brody – the dark-haired voluptuous 20-something star of an upcoming Mitchell Brothers porno movie called *Sodom and Gomorrah: The Last Seven Days* – was "revolutionizing" the erotic arts. In reality, attending and writing about her strip act for the *BARB* was a way of getting in for free. Then came that call from Jack Goff. "Greetings," he said, "do I have a proposition for *you*…"

Goff was a writer of what he euphemistically called "erotic literature" who wanted to take his work to the next level. Books were on the way out, he said. And just what was the wave of the future? Something brand new, Goff explained, something called *cassette tapes*. His proposal: tape one of his dirty books complete with sound effects, package it nicely, then sell it to porno shops and, if possible, the Mitchell Brothers who would distribute it in the lobbies of their theaters.

The big challenge, Goff said, would be finding the right girl to narrate. That girl, he was convinced, was Jacquie Brody. He would offer her five hundred dollars for a weekend's work, plus two percent off the top. What he wanted me to do was help set up the deal. "There'll be some money in it for you too," he promised. So I made the call.

Jacquie agreed to talk, and a meeting was arranged for the next morning. At 10 a.m., Goff and his wife picked me up for the ride. They were an old couple, and an odd one. He had reddish-gray hair and a silver-black beard that he stroked more vigorously than anyone I'd ever seen. Even though he was now bent with age, I could see that he'd once been a handsome man. The wife – whom he called mama – on the other hand, appeared to have *always* been ugly. Sporting an enormous black pimple on her chin with thick hairs protruding from its head, she limped badly and could walk only with an enormous metal cane.

Their vehicle looked almost as old as they were and had been stripped of all accoutrements; I'd never seen a more dilapidated car. "If anybody asks," said Goff, yanking ineffectually on the handle of the door to climb into the driver's seat, "you're the general manager of Jack Goff, Inc., understand? That way they respect you. I know how to deal with these types, believe me, I've been doing it all my life."

"He's done it all his life," Mama Goff chimed in.

The door flew open and Goff almost fell to the pavement, but managed to stabilize himself by grabbing the handle with both hands. I opened the door on the other side to sit shotgun, with Mama Goff in back. Getting her in had been a special challenge, accomplished only by sticking the end of her cane out a window. Goff turned the key and the car coughed, then sputtered to life.

"We don't take no bullshit, understand?" he said. "If they try anything funny, we just walk out. You'd be amazed at the psychological effect of a well-staged walkout." He gave me a lecherous wink. "If we get this thing set up," he said, "we'll have a good time making that tape."

Mama Goff chuckled. "Berkeley must be a pretty swinging town, eh?" she offered. "Last time we was in Berkeley we went to a party, remember Pa?"

"Sure as hell do," said Goff as the lecherous smile that had begun at the corners of his mouth spread upward encompassing his cheeks, then his eyes and finally his entire forehead. Suddenly it changed into a look of disgust. "Man," he said, "we thought it was gonna be a good party, but nobody wanted to swap. Everybody just made it with their own partners, can you believe that?"

"Sounds pretty backward," I averred.

There was too much traffic, and his mood began to change. Twice I offered to drive, and twice he turned me down. He was beginning to breathe hard and sweat was pouring off his forehead. Several times he clutched his chest as if in pain.

"Jack's got a heart condition," Ma Goff confided from the back seat. "Jack, why don't you let David drive?"

"Naw," he said, pulling into the parking lot of a supermarket, "I just need a little rest and I'll be fine." He got out of the car, lumbered to the trunk and returned with a six-pack of Pepsi. "Pepsi opens up his arteries," Mama Goff explained. Jack sat in the driver's seat guzzling Pepsi, and 15 minutes later we were back underway.

Jacquie Brody was dressed up and waiting for us. Her old man, Jason, sat in the kitchen smoking a cigar. After rum and cokes all around, we got right down to business. "I want five hundred bucks on the table," Jacquie announced.

The vessels in Goff's forehead bulged. "Impossible," he said. "What's to keep you from ripping me off, what guarantees do we have?"

"Well what guarantees do *I* have?" Jacquie fired back. "How do I know that you'll pay?"

They sat glaring at each other across the table with beads of sweat rolling down Goff's forehead. "I've got an idea," I put in. "Half when the contract is signed, the other half when the tape is completed."

"You mean when the tape is *accepted*," Goff said.

"*Completion* not acceptance!" Brody said.

"What if I don't like the tape?" Goff yelled. "I haven't even heard you read yet!"

"Well what if I don't like the script?" Brody returned. "I don't know if I even wanna *do* your lousy book!"

Without another word, Goff closed his briefcase, stood up and marched towards the door. The negotiations had begun. Over the next eight hours Goff got up twice more to leave, and twice more was "coaxed" into staying. Once it was established that Brody liked the script and was willing to do it, Goff had her do a reading that came out quite well. Then the money haggles began: to whom would it be transferred, and when? And working conditions: how many hours would be required, where would they be spent and would any sex be involved? Then, what if Goff didn't like the tape; who would own it if rejected?

On and on it went, and the effect on Goff was appalling. After a while he was sweating so profusely that he asked for a handkerchief to wad up in his left hand. Then, as the talks continued, he stroked his beard nonstop with his right hand while mopping his brow with the soaking handkerchief in his left. Twice Mama Goff went out for Pepsis and by the time evening rolled in, his speech was becoming slurred.

Then, miraculously, it was over. The recording session was set for two days hence and everyone departed as friends. The minute we were safely across the Bay Bridge, though, Goff started cursing again. "Fuckin' bitch!" he ranted. "Who does she think she is?"

"For God's sake calm down," Mama Goff urged. "She's young; she thinks she needs to make an impression."

"I dunno," Goff said, his voice thick like soup, "I'm not sure that this will work."

Just then a car whizzed by with its radio blaring and I caught a snatch of President Nixon's voice. "Holy shit," I said, "what time is it? We're missing Nixon's speech." The speech had been announced earlier that day amid rampant speculation that the President, in the wake of the ongoing Watergate scandal, was about to resign. "I've got a TV at home," I said. "You think we can get there fast?"

He stepped on it. I appreciated his good intentions, but a jalopy is still a jalopy. On Telegraph Avenue we passed another car with its radio on and I caught half a sentence: *"To have served in this office is to have felt a sense of kinship with each and every..."*

"Hurry up!" I urged.

"I'm going as fast as I can," Goff groaned. Something about the tone of his voice made me turn. He was mopping his forehead continuously with the porn star's handkerchief, but not fast enough to catch the sweat pouring out from his brow. We raced down Telegraph, then roared around the corner onto Channing Way and stopped in front of my house.

"Come on up," I offered, "and have some Pepsi."

All three of us lumbered out of the car and, with each other's help, made it into my room. Before anybody could sit down, I switched on the TV. The broad shoulders and pinched dark face of Richard Nixon filled the screen. I fiddled with the dial to focus the picture and turned up the volume. *"...and I shall continue to work for the great causes to which I have been dedicated..."* the President was saying.

"Holy shit," I yelled, "he's resigning! Nixon is resigning!"

From the couch behind me came only silence. *"...completely abhorrent to every instinct in my body,"* the man on the screen was saying, *"but as President I must put the interests of the nation first. May God's grace be with you in all the days ahead."*

I managed to take my eyes off the screen long enough to glance back at the Goffs. Jack was sitting on the sofa, but something was wrong. His legs were stretched out in front of him and his head was thrown way back with the mouth gaping wide in the red-puckered face. Mama Goff sat beside him calmly beating his chest with a fist. "Call an ambulance," she said, "I think he's had a heart attack."

I never found out whether the old man lived or died, for within days I too was on my way out. There was simply no way of avoiding the uncomfortable truth any longer: I had had more than enough of this unholy place. It was time, once again, to expand my search.

David Haldane

17.

Mummies

The first thing you see after stepping off a bus in Guanajuato, Mexico, is the gigantic funeral parlor across from the depot. It's a fine one too, with large picture windows in front exhibiting beautiful floral wreaths and a wide selection of cushy coffins inside. The week's special is always displayed front and center, open for potential customers to examine inside and out. And stationed around it, a small army of smiling salesmen stands ready to answer your questions and show you their wares.

For me there are two memorable things about this intriguing place. It symbolizes the town's cottage industry and main tourist draw: a popular collection of mummies. And it was the first place I landed after escaping from the heavenly gateway I once believed Berkeley to be. By the time I left towards the end of 1974, the city had become something far different; a place where things were dying, including the spirit of anyone who stayed there too long. What had once been the exciting capital of a new world being born was now a caricature of itself, a town where the smell of decay was pervasive. So it was somehow fitting that the bus I took *out* had dropped me off *here*.

Guanajuato was not my ultimate destination, of course. That would be San Miguel de Allende, a picturesque little artists' colony where I planned to spend some time writing. In those days the town was known primarily for three things; an art school respected throughout central Mexico; a small independent college called Instituto Allende catering mostly to foreigners like me; and a sizeable community of expat writers and artists who'd taken refuge on the town's benches, balustrades and balconies. Before finding a balcony of my own, however, there were some mummies I wanted to see.

"Hey," I asked a kid in the street, "*donde estan las momias?*" Where are the mummies?

He smiled conspiratorially, as if sharing a dirty little secret, then switched to English and beckoned me forward. "Follow me," he said, and off we went.

The truth is that I've always been fascinated by mummies. Even as a child in Southern California, I had a favorite one at the Los Angeles County Museum of Natural History in Exposition Park. He was in the Egyptian section and I used to hang out with him on Saturday afternoons.

We didn't talk much. But we did do lots of staring; me at him and him at whatever it is inside those bandages that mummies see. For me, in fact, that was the million dollar question; what really *was* inside those bandages? What did he look like, this thing that was once human? What color hair did he have, what shade eyes? Was he smiling? What was the shape of his nose?

I had a standing fantasy in those years. I imagined myself sneaking into the museum after dark, long after the guards had gone, and breaking the glass of the mummy's case. I imagined slowly unraveling its wraps until it lay revealed before me. I imagined myself sitting there, staring at the body, looking at its parts, conjuring up in my mind what it had looked like alive. And imagining what I would look like dead.

It was a childish fantasy, of course; one I soon grew out of, or at least forgot. I thought about more practical things; how to make a living, make an impression, make a woman. The mummy in Los Angeles stayed there, is probably there still; how odd to spend so many decades gathering dust in a sarcophagus under a glass while little boys strip you with their eyes. But my life swept on, as life always does, beyond all caring for its scattered debris; mummies in museums and bodies in parlors. They were nothing but the discarded casings of the human spirit spread like broken bottles in the dumpsters of time.

Then I got to Guanajuato. Following the boy through crowded streets, I felt an uncanny sense of excitement. As we huffed up a hill, a group of other boys gathered around us. "*Las momias, las momias?*" they said, smiling with anticipation. "We give tour – only fifteen pesos!"

"No thank you," I said, but still they followed, pulling little brown objects from their pockets.

"Mummy candy?" one of the boys chimed. He held up a long brown sugary-looking stick of something twisted into the grotesque shape of a screaming mummy. It was shrouded in purple cellophane, barely visible through the wrap. The boy smiled proudly. "Is very good, you see. Only fifty centavos."

And suddenly we were there. The doorway was the front entrance of what looked like a long hallway, perhaps a hundred yards in length, guarded by a little man wearing a big sombrero. He was sitting at a table with a bucket full of coins and a sign reading *Entrada 1 peso.* What genius, I thought; in Guanajuato even the dead still work for the city.

Most of them, I eventually learned, departed this earth during a cholera epidemic in 1833. Entombed in vaults above the ground at the local cemetery, they rested in peace for many years. Then a strange and, in retrospect, wonderful thing happened: the city began collecting an interment tax. Some couldn't afford it and others were disinclined to try. So from 1866 until 1958 when the tax was finally repealed, dead people were disinterred as their relatives fell into arrears. The

Nazis and Nudists

unforeseen bonus: a community of remains, mummified by desert conditions and providentially attractive to tourists.

The attraction was not lost on locals, many of whom found creative ways to cash in. The city's abundance of funeral parlors set the tone. Its commercial district followed suit by offering a variety of mortality-related goods including death masks, black candles and mummy postcards. And young boys added to the general celebratory mayhem by supplying tourists with such unique items the mummy-shaped candies and key chains resembling dead mummy thumbs.

I gave the boy a tip, paid the entry fee and stepped through the door. It was dark inside and I had to pause a moment to let my eyes adjust. When they finally did, I couldn't help but gasp; standing dimly before me, lining both sides of the long hallway like grim palace guards watching over a macabre gallery of death, the mummies of Guanajuato grinned eerily at anyone brave enough to make their acquaintance. They were the center of this town's spectacle, the esteemed silent residents who made it all possible. Some clothed and others naked, they seemed to be laughing at shocked spectators like me as if to say "stare boldly now for your time will come."

I stepped forward and gazed at the first in line, the body of a young man perhaps in his late twenties. Brown and stiff-looking like shoe leather, the skin had shrunken and molded itself neatly around the man's skeleton. His arms were folded over his chest in the traditional attitude of burial, but the face was alive with the mouth hanging wide open like a choir boy's. The eyelids were molded shut over the eyes, the head round and bald and the nose and lips thin slivers of skin. On the man's cheeks, scant once-red hair was all that remained of a light beard of perhaps a few weeks' growth.

My God, I thought, he looks so real. And then I realized that he *was*.

Next I saw a young girl laid out in her coffin, still dressed in what must have been a pretty white gown. She looked about 16 and even now, even after all this, even with sunken eye sockets encasing glazed eyeballs hard as stones, I could tell that she'd been pretty. The next man was thin, and the one after that fat. His skin fell about him like an oversized tunic, like the billowing robes of a Tibetan monk. Then there was a mother with sagging breasts and an old man with a scraggly beard and stooping shoulders. Perhaps he'd been someone's grandpa, perhaps he'd read Cervantes.

Finally there was a shelf of babies with a sign over one proclaiming it "The World's Smallest Mummy." To prove it, the bodyless head of an adult mummy with neatly combed black hair, white teeth and a pretty yellow headband had been placed next to it and, sure enough, outsized the baby by miles. One of the other babies wore a tiny metal crown and the miniature silken robe and yellow cords of a pope or king, like an expensive Christmas doll bought a century ago and long forgotten.

Just then a troupe of Mexican school children paraded by, pointing and laughing at what they saw. I flattened myself against a wall to let them pass and thought of my own childhood, standing before the Egyptian mummy in its great sarcophagus with a look of morbid fascination on my face. The faces of these children showed fascination too, but of a lighter kind. They were amused, closer to death, greeting it as a weird uncle who told funny stories.

I, on the other hand, was frightened of death, facing it only on the confused side streets of nighttime imagery. I had exalted death, viewed it as a dark celebrity who I watched but never met. Now I stared at the long dim line of dead bodies and felt a strange intimacy with them that I had never known. I had seen them in their nakedness, seen them frankly as they were. I had gazed into their eyes and seen my own staring back from those who were what I am and are what I will be. They had shared the naked truth of what we *all* are, swept aside pretentious illusions with glassy honest stares.

I was not the same person who had walked into this place an hour before. For this I was grateful, and at last I understood why the mummies were there. They were there for those who need them, to be seen by those who must.

And so the ghost hunt began.

18.

A Ghost on the Tracks

It was late afternoon by the time we got to the haunted place on the railroad tracks outside of town. There we paused, waiting to see if the ghost would appear. "This is where it happened," my friend Pierre said. "This is where he died."

There is probably a higher per capita population of gringos in San Miguel de Allende than anywhere else in Mexico. It's a quaint town with beautiful colonial-style buildings and cobblestone streets, a birthplace of the Mexican revolution where patriots from throughout the country gather to pay homage to their history each year.

It's also a mecca of sorts, though far less known, to historians of the American counterculture. For there was a time when this town served as a haven for worn out beatniks from San Francisco, the place where they came to escape, the crazy desert hideout where great souls came to rest their squandered hearts. You still see them from time to time; if you suffer from a bit of the madness yourself, sport even an ounce of beatnik blood, they recognize you with a nod. And if you ask them about San Miguel they'll say "yes, this is the place, this is where it came to an end, this is where Neal Cassady walked down the tracks and never returned."

In 1975 my favorite beatnik was a guy named Pierre Delattre who'd published a novel called *Tales of a Dalai Lama* and taught creative writing at Instituto Allende in San Miguel. What interested me more, though, was that he hailed from the Bay Area where the national media had once dubbed him the "beatnik priest." An ordained Presbyterian minister, Pierre had earned that moniker in the 1950s while operating the Bread and Wine Mission, a coffee house ministry catering to troubled beatniks in San Francisco's North Beach. He'd also edited *Beatitude*, a magazine that published some of the earliest works by those progenitors to the hippies. And, as both a counselor and an editor, he'd hobnobbed and shared intimacies with such iconic literary figures as Allen Ginsberg, Richard Brautigan, Lawrence Ferlinghetti and Neal Cassady, to name a few.

Especially tantalizing were my friend's stories about Cassady, who had appeared in Jack Kerouac's classic novel, *On the Road*, as its central character, Dean Moriarty. The book, of course, became the Bible of the beat movement and Cassady, by extension, its Angel Gabriel. Later he joined author Ken Kesey's Merry Pranksters, a band of roving psychedelic-guzzling long-hairs, and became a hippie icon as well.

"Sure I knew Neal," Pierre told me one morning over coffee. "He had his address in my pocket when he died. The police came knocking at my door with Neal's wallet asking whether I knew the guy. 'Well he died out on the railroad tracks,' they said, and that's how I heard the news."

What to Pierre had been news, to me had been lore. I was not of Pierre's generation; for me Neal Cassady was not a person but a literary character, a myth, the embodiment of a new kind of energy. I had come along after Cassady died and, inspired by his legacy, endeavored to further what seemed like his game. But we never made it to the goal post; somewhere along the way we got lost and now wandered bewildered with spectral question marks hanging over our heads like memories of a party we'd been drunk at but couldn't recall. If we could only get it back, even just a glimpse, perhaps we could retrieve the secret. "I want to see where it happened," I told Pierre, so the next day he took me for a walk.

It was the kind of day we loved in Mexico: warm and fraught with potential, the kind of day in which you could smell the countryside; smell where you were; smell the dryness and stillness laced with the threat of chaos just one wisp away. Pierre was wearing a straw hat with an apple seed bag strewn over his shoulder and his big black dog, Nanny, bounding close behind. Together we strode between rows of stone houses heading for the railroad station on the outskirts of town.

"Neal knew lots of people in San Miguel," Pierre said, "so he often came around. He'd been here only a day or two when he died. I didn't even know he was in town."

"What was he like?" I wanted to know.

The beatnik priest reflected. "He was a thin, tattooed, well-muscled man," Pierre said. "He always stood very erect. By 1965 he was speeding like mad and drinking too much; that's the combination that finally killed him. He told friends he was going out to count the railroad ties to Celaya."

We had reached the train station, a strange little village of boxcars with flowerpots hanging from their sides. A toothless brown mother sat in the doorway of one of the boxcars suckling a baby surrounded by ragged young children. "*Adios,*" said Pierre, waving his hand, and from the mother and children came the reply, "*adios, adios* – go with God." Then we were walking down the tracks toward Celaya. It was so hot that the rails were steaming, and I had to shade my eyes.

"Neal was a showoff," Pierre said, "but in a marvelous sort of way. He'd just start rapping and everybody would sit there listening for hours. The connections went all over the world from politics, to art, to music, to literature – they covered a wide gamut. He was like a vast connecting circuit, you could see these synapsis connecting in his head."

Pierre and I walked on in silence for a time. The landscape was excruciatingly bright and as I glanced down at the track I began to count its ties. *One, two, three, four, five, six, seven…*

"To me the most interesting thing about that period," Pierre said, "was that there were two directions we were going. One was to slow down – getting into the slowness of stone – and the other was to speed up, just ride with it and go as fast as you could. Neal was into kind of a frantic, speedy attempt to arrive at the end which, of course, is death."

Twentythirtyfortyfifty...

"He was a guy who caught the speed of our time," Pierre said as we quickened our pace. "He was like a jet plane trying to break the sound barrier. The first planes that tried it exploded in the air, but finally they managed to crack the sound barrier and push off into complete silence."

I was trying hard to listen, but beneath me the railroad ties were moving so fast that they looked like a line. "Neal went faster and faster," Pierre said. "He was like a racer driving his car against a wall hoping that, by crashing through, he could get to the other side where death is not a problem."

Sixhundredsevenhundredeighthundredninehundred... "This is it," Pierre said and he stopped.

For me it was a head-on collision; the railroad ties I'd been counting tumbled out of me like building blocks and there were numbers all over the countryside. We were standing on a little bridge by a switch where two tracks joined. For a few moments, we stood in silent reverence pierced only by the whoosh of the wind rustling dryly through the desert moving Pierre's hair even under his hat.

"I came out here two weeks after he died," my friend said finally. "I wanted to feel if there was anything left of him hanging around, but there wasn't at all because he'd already taken off. Neal wanted to take off in the worst way."

I gazed out over the sand and knew with certainty that my search would go on. With Cassady gone, there was no reason for me to stick around either. I thought about it a moment longer, and then made my choice; like the ghost of a long-dead beatnik, I too would soon take off.

David Haldane

19.

Druggies with Knives

Shivering in the courtyard of a dilapidated Guatemalan house about to be murdered by drug-crazed thieves, it occurred to me one night that what I needed was a wife. That's when I really knew that it was time to go home. At the moment, though, there was a more immediate challenge: how to evade their murderous knives. Let me roll this back a week: it all started when some friends dragged me out of San Miguel on a day that the banks were closed.

I didn't know they were closed, of course. All I knew was that we were taking an unplanned vacation to the south. "Jack is cool," a co-traveler had said regarding the man whose house we were supposedly visiting in Antigua, Guatemala. "I'm sure that he'll let us crash."

"But I've got to get some money," I complained, caught off guard.

"Don't worry," my friend said, "we'll front you whatever you need."

So he, his wife and I took off down the Mexican Federal Highway. Taking turns driving their '67 Dodge Van, we spent three days on the road, stopping at every quaint village we saw. My favorite was a place called *Juchitan* where the women worked hard while the men sat around drinking beer.

Finally we knocked at the door of a large house in downtown Antigua paid for, I was told, by the owner's earnings from a cooper mine nearby. "Who's *he*?" Jack asked, pointing straight at me. After hearing my friend's (rather meager, I must say) explanation, he made a grimace that I didn't much like. So sorry, our would-be host said, but he'd already had houseguests for a week and really didn't need any more. "Perhaps another time," he said, glancing briefly at me. So my companions, who mysteriously *did* have permission to stay, quickly bid me adieu. In one week's time, they promised, they would meet me in a town thirty miles to the north called Panajachel. "I'm going to need some money," I stammered, feeling very uncomfortable.

My friend smiled warmly, dug into his pocket and fished out fifty quetzals which, at the time, amounted to about $6.50 US. "It's cheap there," he said, "you won't need very much. You can pay us back in San Miguel." Then he patted my shoulder, smiled again, this time a little awkwardly I thought, and suddenly I was alone. For a few hours I wandered around the strange town I'd never seen. Then, finally finding the bus terminal, exchanged most of the cash for a ticket, climbed aboard a carriage and settled down for the two-hour ride.

My memory of the week that followed is a haze of vague impressions punctuated by two distinct ones. The first is of a beggar wandering through Panajachel's public market with a scarf on his head and hideous scars on his cheeks. His problem, someone told me: an advanced case of leprosy. The second and final impression is of the utter, impenetrable darkness at an open-air encampment of vagrants where, lacking funds for a hotel, I had given some criminal my last quetzals for the right to sleep.

The guy who'd taken the money was a small bearded American resembling Charles Manson, even to the inexplicably maniacal gleam all but spurting from his eyes. "Keep an eyelid parted," he'd advised after collecting his fee. "There are some bad dudes here who'd happily gut you like a pig just for your clothes." His smile did nothing to ease the unnerving sense that he was offering a preview of his own well-considered plan. Arriving at the spot to which he'd directed me, however, I soon forgot all about the scary little man.

It looked like the remnants of a building destroyed long ago, a shamble of beams and half walls connected by the skeleton of what once was. I laid out my sleeping bag in an open courtyard among crumbling walls and took in the scene as darkness fell. That's when I saw the lights. At first there were just a few, darting around like a family of fireflies. Then their numbers increased until the family was a tribe, and the tribe became a swarm. As my eyes adjusted, I could see what they were: the flickering of matches and glow of pipes as a gang of homeless dopers prepared for the night. Their shadows danced large on the low walls like the exaggerated ghosts in every bad horror movie I'd ever seen.

I decided to take the little man's advice by keeping one eye open. Before devising a strategy to do so, however, I was struck by an unsettling thought: that I could die here tonight. That I could die and no one would ever know where I was or what had happened to me. My mother would probably put an ad in some obscure Mexican newspaper inquiring about her lost son, but no one would ever respond. Perhaps one day she and my dad would randomly speculate about the life that never was. The idea made me shudder. And that's when I started thinking about wives.

I realized that I had reached a crossroads. Behind me was the crazy zany colorful unpredictable ecstatic and ultimately terrifying journey of the young. Up ahead, assuming that I didn't get murdered tonight, well, who knew? A wife, a family, a house? Whatever form it took, I knew it would be home. Because that's what I needed and that's what I'd get; a green leafy space of my own.

People don't believe me when I tell them how I met my first wife. By the the time it happened I was back in Long Beach after having, by what I took to be a miracle, somehow evaded the mean blades of Guatemala. A few days after seeing their glint, I had even hooked up with my two treacherous friends with whom I had returned to San Miguel and, eventually, to the United States where my mother, frankly, didn't seem all that pleased to see me. Perhaps it was because, in our first conversation, I asked her for money.

But she was my mom, after all, and willing to forgive. That fact became obvious a few weeks later when she gave me a call. "David," she said, her German accent unusually thick. "Promise me you *von't* be mad."

"What did you do, Mom?"

"I put you an ad in the paper."

I immediately knew what she meant. Ever since my return, Mom – apparently taking my musings about settling down to heart – had been fretting that her 20-something son with literary pretensions had no gainful employment and, worse, no wife. The ad read: *Young writer, 26, seeks bubbly spontaneous female for fun and companionship.*

At first I was more amused than angry; the deed, after all, had been done. Its full impact, however, didn't hit me until 6:30 the next morning when I was awakened by the first of many calls. "Hey," a female voice demanded, "are you the guy with the ad in the paper?"

"What if I am?" I responded, off-balance.

And so it went, day after day. My mother had been so pessimistic regarding my ability to attract women, even with her help, that she'd taken the ad out for a two-week run. Those weeks were delightful, but enervating; I'd never have guessed how many bubbly spontaneous – yet still available – females lived in Southern California.

A woman with a Ph.D. called to complain that she sorely lacked intellectual stimulation. Several unpublished women writers read me their favorite stories. One young caller phoned three times, from three different cocktail lounges, to announce that she'd just run away from an overbearing mother and wondered whether I'd join her for a drink. Another woman told me that her canary talked to her; still another that she heard voices at night. And a third, who conceded to being in her 50s, wanted to discuss the finer points of ballroom dancing.

The only way I could get any sleep was to take the phone off the hook, which I did regularly after returning from a night on the town.

That ad, as you can imagine, landed me lots of dates. In fact, for the first time ever, my supply of dinner and movie partners greatly exceeded the demand. To avoid chaos, I devised a simple questionnaire for use whenever the telephone rang. After asking each woman a series of basic questions, I'd take a phone number and tell her that I might be getting back.

Every night for those two sweetly grueling weeks, I went out with a different woman. A few were interesting; one was intriguing enough to eventually become my wife. It was well into the second week that I heard from Dawn. Actually, to be strictly honest, it wasn't her I heard from but a friend of hers named Louise. We chatted pleasantly for half an hour before she announced, "Listen, I'm not calling for myself but for a friend who'd love to meet you. At least I *think* she would. For heaven's sake, though, don't tell her about the ad."

So Louise told Dawn that she'd met me at a seminar and, with a little urging, arranged a blind date. After that – there's simply no other way of putting it – it was infatuation at first sight. Not, however, without its challenges. The first one came just four months later when, reading the newspaper together at her apartment one Sunday, Dawn suddenly began to laugh. "Listen to this," she said, and proceeded to read aloud a particularly salacious ad from the personals section of the classifieds. "Hey," she said with a mischief in her eyes, "let's call this guy and give him Louise's number."

"Dawn," I said, choosing my words very carefully, "there's something you ought to know..."

My future wife nearly left me that night. In fact, she did; for about 24 hours. In that interval, Dawn later told me, she did lots of soul searching. She also polled numerous girlfriends on the question of whether it was advisable to stay with a man who'd deceived her in such a humiliating way. She'd thought she knew me, Dawn told them, but really, she now admitted I "could be the Boston Strangler." In the end she decided that it was at least *tolerable,* even if not altogether wise, to stick around, an outcome that brought me relief.

Sometime later, after we had become an almost-boring married couple and I'd partially realized my mother's dream of gainful employment by accepting a part-time job in the classified advertising department of our local newspaper, the ultimate irony occurred; I met the woman who'd taken that ad.

"I remember it clearly," she told me, "because it seemed awfully weird for a mother to be calling it in."

I think I must have smiled with something resembling gratitude. And instinctively knew that it was time to get on with life.

David Haldane

20.

Wading into the Mainstream

Four years later, in 1982, I was standing in a yard near Riverside, California, watching a 25-foot cross burst into flames.

It wasn't spontaneous combustion; the ignition had been sparked by dozens of white-hooded figures wielding butane torches. As the flames lit up the night, two distinct soundtracks could be heard. Inside the fenced space, the ghosts surrounding me let out eerie cheers. Outside, where a crowd of neighbors had gathered to jeer, an 8-year-old child began to cry.

"There, there," the little girl's mother said, stroking her hair, "everything will be all right."

How I ended up stuck in a yard controlled by the Invisible Knights of the Ku Klux Klan is a long and convoluted story. Like so many others – including the one recounting my marriage – it began indirectly with a call. This time, though, it was *me* initiating the contact instead of some lonely woman in a bar. The recipient was James Phelan, a well-known journalist whose book, *Howard Hughes: the Hidden Years*, had just made the cover of *Time Magazine*. I was calling to ask for an interview, a request to which he graciously assented.

"When you pitch the piece," Phelan said in the gravelly voice that would become familiar, "tell them it's an exclusive. This is the only magazine interview I'm going to give."

And just like that I was in the big time. Or so I thought. The interview appeared in the June, 1977, issue of *Penthouse Magazine*, my first sale to a national publication. Before I could even raise a glass in celebration, however, my new wife sat me down for a talk.

The problem, she said, was that I just wasn't carrying my weight; while she was bringing in the cash, I was still just digging for scratch. So here was the deal: I had until my 30th birthday – roughly two years hence – to get on board, or she would be forced to "seriously re-evaluate our relationship." In other words, unless I got motivated about acquiring the full-time gainful employment my mother craved, I would soon find myself sexless and single. That's when, in what has to be considered a timeless ode to the success of a mother's scheming, I decided to try daily journalism.

It was easier said than done. The editors of large newspapers, I soon discovered, would not even deign to talk to someone with no daily experience. And those overseeing the smaller local sheets didn't consider alternative journalism – or *Penthouse Magazine*, for that matter – to be any kind of experience at all. So it was back to knocking on doors.

Gradually I developed a pitch. "Gosh," I told the publisher of an obscure 7,000-circulation daily in Downey, California, who I took to be a conservative Republican, "I've wasted so much time writing for left-wing rags. Now I just want to settle down and prove that I can handle a *real* job." Translation: *I'm a poor reformed schlep-of-a-hippy who's finally seen the light and needs a savior like you.* In retrospect, it wasn't that far from the truth.

In any case, it worked: he hired me, and for the first time in my life I had to start wearing ties. I'll spare you the gritty details of the next several years. Suffice it to say that I quickly became acquainted with a species I have since learned is endemic to the grungy world of newspaper journalism: the borderline psychotic, bipolar newsroom tyrant. Though every newspaper harbors some variant of the species, these little Mussolini types are especially prevalent at smaller papers where they swoop down into the newsroom (or worse, call reporters into glass-paneled offices) to berate them in front of their peers. It has always escaped me how anyone thinks this could improve newsroom performance; any victim with even a semblance of mental health eventually reacts by leaving the industry. As I didn't fall into that category, I quickly adopted an alternative strategy: moving on to a different tormentor. One thing led to another, friends spoke to friends and, after a brief sojourn at another hell-hole in West Covina, I found myself at the *Riverside Press-Enterprise* where, in 1982, I met the KKK.

They were already a fringe group by then, a bunch of wannabe champions of white Christian virtue who saw their sacred duty as protecting America from the burgeoning onslaught of non-white, atheistic hordes. As one of three feature writers at the PE, my job was to write about things I found interesting in Riverside County. And, perhaps because of my own off-center background, I found fringe groups extremely interesting. Lots, of course, had been written over the years about the Klan, which had long since passed its heyday. What struck me as new was that nearly half of its members were women.

So I began hanging out with them, interviewing female adherents and, on one particularly memorable evening, watching them burn a very large cross in a very small yard. What I learned was surprising: that the women of the Klan were not that different from women everywhere; housewives, mothers, secretaries and clerks. And that, like those other women (and, for that matter, men) they were concerned about the safety of their children, the bad economy, increasing violence in their lives and the quality of American education. What was different was that they had embraced a uniquely abhorrent way of expressing those concerns.

"It's great to get them in," California Klan organizer Mike Cook told me, adding that their increased visibility was part of an effort to sanitize the organization's public image. "Women are traditionally nonviolent. They draw new members; people see women in the Klan and they want to join."

Yet just coming into their yard, for me, was a disconcerting experience. For starters I had to pass through a gate adorned by a cardboard sign reading *Whites Only*. One of the protesters later told me she had been denied entry after a Klansman noticed the Star of David dangling on her chest; I sincerely hoped that they hadn't noticed mine. And as I stood in that yard feeling scorched by hot flames and listening to the plaintive sobs of a frightened child, I couldn't escape the sensation of being in some hellish scene from Dante on the wrong side of an unholy divide.

I had no intention, however, of crossing back over. Because to do so, I instinctively understood, would be a surrendering of something even more sacred than my personal sensibilities, more important than how I felt about the people I accompanied or the twisted ideology they shared. This was about a higher calling; one that, I believed in my youthful exuberance, dwarfed all others. I had been given a front-row seat (quite a step up from the sixteenth or seventeenth I'd occupied in college) at an unfolding that few were privileged to view, an event that would be taking place with or without my presence. *With* my presence, however, came something more: the added witness of those who read the newspaper I served. At least that's what I told myself. And so I bit my lip and contemplated what a grand life this would be.

Meanwhile another process was secretly unfolding that would have a profound impact on my life and career. It had begun back when I was still the protégé of James Phelan whose sponsorship, it turned out, would help me in mysterious and indirect ways. One day he called with an interesting tip: a Bay Area group called People's Temple had moved to Guyana where they were living like brainwashed zombies under the dictatorial rule of a weird minister named Jim Jones. Phelan knew this, he said, because a group of concerned relatives and defectors had contacted him with the story.

"They say they can get me into the camp to see for myself," he said. But he was bogged down on another project and wondered whether I might pursue this one in his stead. My response was immediate and heartfelt: are you kidding? So he gave me the contacts and I started making calls.

Eventually I pitched the story to *Playboy Magazine* where the response was less than enthusiastic: *zombies in the jungles of Guyana, really? Yeah, right.* A few weeks later, Jonestown was international front page news.

The historic event that put it there was triggered by the fact that I wasn't the only one to whom the relatives were talking. They had also contacted Rep. Leo Ryan, a U.S. congressman from a suburb near San Francisco, who organized a fact-finding tour. On November 18, 1978, the delegation was attacked by gun-toting Jim Jones followers who mowed down the Congressman, several journalists and some of the defectors accompanying them. Then, in the largest mass suicide of modern history, more than nine hundred Jonestown residents drank poisoned Kool-Aid and died.

I've often wondered what would have happened had I been on that plane: probably the ignominious end to a very short career. As it was, I got two phone calls the morning the story broke. One was from Phelan, who wanted his stuff back. The other was from a *Long Beach Press Telegram* reporter asking for a source or two. My decision to accommodate him turned out to be career-changing; the reporter wrote a prize-winning story that earned him a trip to Guyana from where he wrote several more. Those dispatches, in turn, got him hired by the venerable *Los Angeles Times* where one day he would return my favor in a manner that was quite spectacular.

The moral: no matter what anyone tells you, don't bother planning for the future because it all comes down to chance. It was a lesson soon to be driven home in a life-changing way.

21.

Seizing the Times

I was sitting at my desk at the *Press Enterprise* one morning when the heavens parted and the hand of God reached down to tap me on the shoulder. "This is Bob Rawitch," a voice on the telephone said. "I'd like to talk to you about a job."

Rawitch was editor of the *Los Angeles Times'* suburban sections which, in those days, were the main portal through which new hires entered the hallowed sanctums of Southern California's largest and most respected newspaper. For years I'd been dutifully sending him resumes and receiving printed "don't call us we'll call you" letters in return, so working there wasn't exactly a priority. Yet here he was at the end of the line.

"Yes Mr. Rawitch," I said. "Of course I'd like to talk."

The interview lasted two hours. Rawitch and I met over lunch in the elegant executive dining room decorated with original Picassos at the newspaper's Times Mirror Square headquarters in downtown Los Angeles. When it was over I felt I'd done well, but didn't dare be too optimistic. "I'll be in touch," is all Rawitch would say.

Back in the more modest digs of the *Press Enterprise*, word quickly spread. The last PE reporter to go to the *Times* had done so seven years before, so someone being seriously considered was big news. As the story spread among my colleagues, however, it gradually evolved. What had begun as "Haldane's been interviewed by the *Times*" slowly morphed into "He's been hired." It didn't get *really* uncomfortable, though, until people started offering their congratulations.

So two weeks after the interview, I made an emergency call. "Mr. Rawitch, people are starting to congratulate me, and I don' know what to tell them." His answer was immediate and direct. "Tell them thank you," he said. "When can you start?"

I later heard tales of how it had happened, though none were ever confirmed. My favorite: the former *Press Telegram* reporter I'd befriended in the wake of Jonestown was standing at a urinal taking a piss in the third floor men's room when Bob Rawitch sidled up next to him. "Hey," Rawitch casually inquired unzipping his pants, "what do you think of David Haldane?"

"Good man," the guy said zipping up his, "you should definitely give him a try."

And so it came to pass that several weeks later I found myself sipping cocktails aboard a yacht called Summer Mist. Cruising along the shore of Lake Michigan enjoying breathtaking views of the Chicago sunset with me were the representatives of 40 national organizations and a handful of dignitaries from Long Beach, California. The dignitaries' mission: to persuade these best-prospect attendees of America's largest annual gathering of meeting and convention planners to plan their meetings and conventions in Long Beach. Mine: to observe and write about it for the *Los Angeles Times*.

"It's beautiful," one of the targeted meeting planners said, staring over the railing at the fading lights. She was nursing a chilled glass of Perrier between munches of crab salad in pea pods and cucumber briquettes supplied by waitresses bearing silver trays. A few days earlier when I'd called the newspaper's travel office to arrange for an airline ticket, they'd had only one question: tourist or first class? Wow, I thought, resisting the strong urge to pinch my own cheek, this is something I could get used to.

Whatever you get used to, though, life usually finds a way to intrude. For me that happened on a Sunday morning shortly after my return from Chicago as I crouched pulling weeds in the yard. "Your mother has experienced a setback," the nurse on the telephone said, speaking in wide even tones. "You should come to the hospital immediately, but don't drive too fast." Half an hour later I was holding my brother's hand gazing at our mother's corpse.

Diagnosed with advanced lung cancer just three months before, she lay on a table in the intensive care unit with a tube sticking out of her throat. Despite her initial objections, it had been placed there to help her breathe. Those objections, stemming from a deep-seated distaste at the prospect of wearing scarves to hide a hole in her throat, had finally been overcome by a cute young Jewish oncologist who looked deeply into her eyes.

Truth be told, we had a selfish reason for wanting Mom to stick around; her first grandchild – our baby girl – was expected to enter the world screaming in just two months. Instead, Mom *left* it screaming and, well, that was that.

Losing something you're used to is never much fun, but this loss was especially hard. Even though my mother and I had a strained relationship, particularly in the latter years, I always felt a strong emotional connection to her. And, in one of life's great ironies, it was Mom's derailed life that, in some ways, had inspired my own life's hunt for that long-lost rail, the thing I believed would finally provide some semblance of peace and stability. But here's another of life's ironies: the pain of losing something familiar is sometimes be mitigated by the arrival of something new. In my case that happened nine weeks later with the birth of my daughter who I wasn't used to at all.

We called her Adina, the closest Hebrew equivalent to her grandmother's name, Adele. I'll never forget the first time I held her in my arms. As I stared intently into the little face I'd never seen, her mouth formed a perfect circle and I knew that life would proceed.

22.

Small Dark Rooms

The first thing I noticed at the 1350 Club was an abundance of naked men wearing towels. The second thing were the sex orgies on TV screens in every room. "Welcome," the attendant said, winking as he handed me a key. "Please claim your locker and take off your clothes."

By the mid-1980s most people knew about Acquired Immune Deficiency Syndrome – more popularly known as AIDS – and understood something of how it was spread. That was a far cry from just a few years earlier when, still at the *Press Enterprise*, I had met my first victim of this horrible scourge. He was airman first class Raymond Orsini who had contracted the Air Force's then-only-known case and was fighting for the medical benefits he'd been denied. Meeting with him at the small mobile home he occupied near Palm Springs in what turned out to be his final interview, I remember declining a proffered glass of water for fear of catching the disease.

Things had improved somewhat since then; at least now we understood that you couldn't get it from sharing a cup. But the number of infections was increasing and public agencies were scrambling to cope. It was in this atmosphere that the *Times* sent me to do a story on Long Beach's only gay bath house, a place that local health officials had threatened to close.

If you've never been to a bath house, the thing that kicks you in the teeth right off is the necessity of getting naked. God knows I'd done it before, but this was a far cry from the Greek beach I'd spent months prancing around on. For one thing these were all *men*, so it was with some trepidation that I peeled off my clothes. Almost immediately the attention began. "Hey dude," a similarly unadorned young man said, "what's going' on?"

"Well, umm," I stammered, "this is my first time, can you tell me how it works?"

What I really was asking was whether the place was a hotbed of unsafe sex. The question was relevant because the club had refused to follow a city order to open up a cluster of small dark rooms that health officials considered erotic hazards. The club's position was that removing the doors from those rooms would violate its patrons' right to privacy. The city's response: do it anyway or you're gone.

The man who'd called me dude was the first of many to whom I spoke. But taking notes surreptitiously is difficult when you're dressed in a towel. So after each conversation, I'd steal back to the notebook in my locker and frantically write it all down.

At the office next day my editor asked how it went. "Great," I said, "this is a good story. I talked to plenty of people who told me lots of stuff." She had a question: "Did you tell them that you're a reporter?" My blank stare must have said it all. "Well go back," she said, "and do it again."

I returned that very night. Everything was as it had been. Only this time, after creeping into a conversation with someone, I'd casually slip in "Hey, you're not going to believe this, but I'm actually a *Los Angeles Times* reporter doing a story. Would you mind talking?"

It was truly astounding how many didn't mind at all. "I come here for sex if they're cute," one guy told me, adding that he made the trip two or three times a week. But wasn't he afraid of catching AIDS? "Naw," he said, "I can tell if someone's sick just by looking."

Before publishing the story I made one more visit, this time calling the owner in advance. Boy what a difference; where earlier there'd been gay porn, now there were children's cartoons. And even better, nobody asked me to take off my clothes.

After the story appeared, Club 1350 promptly closed. Three months later it was back; this time in the nearby City of Wilmington, California. Naturally, I wanted to do another story. Not surprisingly, they wouldn't let me in. In truth it didn't matter because very soon I would be living a whole new story of my own involving a beach-going guru who would change the trajectory of my life.

• • •

His name was Yogeesh, but it wasn't his teachings that led me astray. A 32-year-old Jain monk from India who lived in an ashram overlooking the ocean, Yogeesh was a respected teacher, healer and spiritual leader. He was also a philanderer and seducer of women who had impregnated one of his followers. That's the part that got me in trouble.

It all started as a simple profile. I visited the ashram, listened to its residents sing and chant and talked to Yogeesh about meditating on the beach. Then I met the former devotee who claimed to be carrying his child. "He taught me tantric yoga," she explained, speaking of a sexual yoga that involves intercourse but isn't supposed to include male ejaculation. "He must have done it wrong."

After conferring, my editor and I decided to downplay that rather dramatic revelation. So I wrote the piece as planned, a fairly glowing portrait with only a passing reference to the alleged impropriety thrown in near the end. That's all it took for the proverbial excrement to hit the spinning blades; a day after the article appeared, a copy of it had been placed on every doorstep in the neighborhood with the offending paragraph underlined in red. That's also when my phone started ringing; apparently the pregnant woman wasn't the only one who felt she'd been betrayed. "I never knew there were so many others," a victim complained.

One of the calls came from a young lady named Joy who, like the

Nazis and Nudists

rest, had been the guru's paramour. Unlike them, however, she also developed an inexplicable liking for *me*. A little over two weeks after my initial piece appeared, a loud meeting at the ashram sealed the errant monk's fate. Present were more than 40 angry neighbors, several with complaints; a community activist railing against the sexual exploitation of vulnerable women; a local police lieutenant who said he was looking into the matter; and Mahendra S. Jain, lay president of the Los Angeles chapter of the International Mahaviv Jain Mission which Yogeesh represented.

"If people don't like him," Jain said, "he cannot stay."

So Yogeesh was sent back to India. And this time his alleged improprieties were in the *Times*' headline instead of just a nuanced paragraph near the end: *Monk Alters Indian Precepts to Fit: Jainism with a West Coast Accent* had become *Devotees Complain: Monk Loses Position after Sex Allegations*. What no one knew, though, was that an even more ironic development had occurred: one of the disgraced monk's girlfriends had become the crusading reporter's. Thus, in the space of two weeks, I lost the moral high ground. Though I didn't yet know it, this would mark the beginning of a long slow descent into darkness and dissolution.

Joy was about ten years younger; a pretty blond who was extremely bright and exceedingly shy. We quickly developed a pattern. I'd call her every afternoon, and once a week – usually on Fridays – go to her apartment for an extended "lunch." It's amazing what rationalizations you come up with to justify nefarious behavior: "It doesn't mean anything and will be over in a minute; I could stop this any time I want; it's not affecting my marriage at all;" and, my favorite and the most self-deceiving: "It's making my marriage better by keeping me sexually satisfied."

All of these, of course, were lies. In my case, they served their purpose by keeping my conscience at bay for more than three years. As time went on, however, leading a double life became increasingly difficult. I began running out of untruths, not only to tell my wife but to tell myself. Keeping track of all the alibis became a herculean task. And, perhaps most distressing, it became more and more difficult to feign passion at home where it no longer lived.

In the end I got caught by my own carelessness. One Saturday morning after hearing Dawn drive off, I broke one of my cardinal rules by calling Joy from the house. My home office in those days was a small room at the top of a spiral staircase. It was from there that I unburdened myself about the troubles in my marriage. And it was from there, upon hanging up, that I realized with horror that my life was about to change; Dawn had returned unannounced and was standing beneath the stairs.

"I heard everything," she said. "How long has this been going on?"

"Three months," I lied.

Then, I swear to God, she fainted. I had never actually seen someone faint. It looked exactly like it does in the movies except for one detail: It lasted less than three seconds. Which meant that when she woke up I was still standing there, having had insufficient time to escape. As it would again years later in a boat off the Philippines, my life rumbled past me like a slow-moving train. "Come with me," Dawn said, "we need to go outside."

Standing in the front yard safely out of the children's' view, she looked me squarely in the eye. "Take off your glasses," Dawn ordered. Then my wife of 15 years punched me hard in the nose. Thirty seconds later she was screeching off in her car and I was wiping blood from my face.

By then we had two children, a girl and a boy, both too young to understand what was happening. So I packed them into their coats and took them to a neighborhood park. As they played on the slide, I watched from a bench with only one thought in mind; that life as I'd known it would never be the same.

23.

Looking Toward the Light

Two weeks later, I was lost in an underwater cavern. Once again it happened in Mexico, this time on the floor of a jungle near Akumal. Truth is, I'd expected to be there with my wife; tickets had been purchased and friends had been told. But now our marriage was ending and the bottom of my world had dropped out. The awful feeling of panicked fear and foreboding that gripped my heart as her car sped off had not gone away. Yet in the midst of depression, I decided to make the Mexican dive trip anyway believing, I suppose, that the diversion would do me good.

I had started scuba diving at 16 and, over the years, had seen it all. I had glided through the dancing kelp forests of Southern California; spotted the dim vision of a shipwreck in the Florida Keys; plunged ecstatically into an underwater canyon in the Cayman Islands; and encountered a shark in Hawaii. One thing I had never experienced, though, was a *cenote*: one of those dark mystical ponds in the jungle, the mirage-of-a-swimming-hole that shouldn't be there. I had heard that some of them opened up into awesomely beautiful underwater caverns and found that intriguing.

The sense of foreboding was still with me as I stepped off the airplane and shuffled alone into the Cancun airport from where I would take a bus to the small coastal town of Akumal. As a diver, I had been taught to stay out of the water during times of emotional turmoil, that panic is the number-one enemy of survival underwater.

Nonetheless, I told myself, this experience would serve as a demarcation between the past and the future; a way, I hoped, to help me move on. I turned out to be right, but in ways I never imagined.

It was cold the day we arrived at the cenote in the Yucatan jungle. Our group of divers – none of whom I'd met before – was accompanied by a local guide. I remember struggling to put on my wetsuit, shivering with excitement tinged with the subtle anticipation of gloom to which I had grown accustomed. The cenote looked like a glassy pond surrounded by mossy rocks outlined by palm trees. Slowly, tentatively, we swam out to its center and descended.

At the bottom, thirty feet down, we paused to gaze at the otherworldly mineral formations adorning the walls. The first thing that struck me was the quality of the light. It was weird, eerie, somehow ethereal. In front of us lay a wide cavern. Entering its mouth, we swam toward the back wall where the cavern narrowed into a small dark tunnel snaking deeply into the earth. The tunnel entrance was marked by rusty metal signs in Spanish. *Peligro* – one warned – Danger, and the other; *No Pase Adelante* – Do Not Proceed!

Legend has it that the ancient Mayans used *cenotes* to make human sacrifices. Staring at those ominous signs illuminated by the beam of my light, I wondered whether any cadavers lay in the tunnel beyond. Then I shuddered and, sucking hard on my regulator, decided to keep the exit in sight.

We swam to the ceiling of the cavern. There, cut into the rock as if honed by some ancient hand, a small indentation burrowed upward. One of the other divers, a young man who'd been here before, stuck his head in the hole and motioned me to follow. I did, and was shocked to find my face above water; a dank air pocket with room for just two heads. Grinning, the man spat out his regulator and looked me in the eye. "Is this cool, or what?" His voice, bouncing off the pressing walls, was disembodied and muffled as if it were coming from inside a coffin. I pulled out my regulator and responded, "Very cool!"

But the voice was not mine. It was the small, distant sound of a man in a bottle. A man caught in a place he shouldn't be, struggling to control the rising wave of dread that, until now, had been willfully kept at bay. I stuffed the regulator back into my mouth and slid out of the hole to the bottom of the cavern. Then it happened. My fins must have stirred up the silt on the floor of the cenote, because suddenly I was enveloped in a blinding cloud.

Frantically I tried to keep my bearings, tried to keep the light of the cavern opening in view. But as the silt billowed all around me, it became increasingly difficult. For what seemed like an eternity, I peered into nothingness, determined not to move my eyes from the spot where the exit had been. Then, with a sinking feeling, realized that I no longer knew the way out.

Panic. It growled at me, baring its gnarly teeth. Every pore of me wanted to bolt, to escape, to swim frantically in the direction I had last seen the light. The only thing stopping me was the knowledge that I could just as easily be rushing toward my death in the dark. They tell you about panic in dive class. Don't give in to it, they say. The solution is simple, really. Stop. Breath. Think. Act. And so began the voice of reason, more of a whimper than a shout.

Don't move, the voice told me, and I froze. *Think*, it said, and I tried to figure my way out. Silt rises and so it must fall. For about as long as it would take someone to drown, I hung there, totally alone, my guts churning with only the sound of my own breathing as evidence that I was alive. Then, as quickly as the cloud had enveloped me, it disappeared and once again I could see my way clear.

After that, the lesson of the dive – indeed, of *all* dives – became a mantra for me, a metaphor for what was happening in my life: Stay calm, don't bolt. Keep your eyes in the direction of the light, even if you can't see it, and have faith that one day you will see it again.

• • •

On the other hand, who has the patience to wait? There's something awesome about the sight of a six-foot-tall black stripper wearing fishnet stockings. And awe is an experience that cannot be denied. Some time later as I gazed worshipfully up at her perfect dark skin, she placed both hands on her hips and shimmied toward the $5 bill I'd hoisted toward her in praise. "Thank you daddy," she said, and I knew right away that I'd be seeing her again.

By then the wounds of divorce had begun to fester with the blood coagulating around jagged holes in the flesh. It is only in retrospect, of course, that I can say that at the time it felt like healing. It had been many months since my encounter with darkness in the cave and, frankly, the silt had not yet settled into the abyss that was my life. But I was anxious to move on and so, having lost my bearings, began hanging out at strip clubs. It was at one of those that I met Hennessy.

She told me she was named after an alcoholic beverage: the one her father had been drinking on the day that she was born. Like the drink, she was bold. She was also loud, funny, sexy, flamboyant – and several inches taller than me. Her other qualities, I would eventually learn, included a deep anger and resentment toward men, severe mood swings, profound emotional instability and a meanness that could jump out at the crack of a whip. In light of her physical attributes, however, all of that paled. And so, near the beginning of a new century, thus also began my new life as a sugar daddy.

It is hard to explain why a middle-aged man with children and a career would adopt a stripper decades younger as his protégé. Not that I was the first to take such a plunge. Still, it was a radical move by anyone's standards and bound to attract some negative attention. The only explanation I can offer is simple narcissism, the kind we see every day. I had succumbed to it once and paid the price with my marriage; why not just take it the rest of the way?

So Hennessy moved in, much to the chagrin of my former wife and kids, and for a time everything seemed grand. Once she accompanied me to my son's Bar Mitzvah where he publically introduced her to the entire assemblage of family and friends as "my dad's girlfriend." Then she lit a candle in his honor. Years later, Dawn confessed that it took her months of therapy to recover.

I even escorted my statuesque companion to the 2000 *Times'* annual banquet at the downtown Bonaventure Hotel, the paper's fancy equivalent of the Academy Awards. She asked for an introduction to the top editor and I complied, though never having met him myself. I have to admit immensely enjoying the poor man's struggle to keep his eyes off my date's ample bosom; perhaps my revenge for receiving no award.

And, of course, there were the parties. Dozens of them, ranging from benign costume balls at nudist resorts to the more serious swingers' conventions in Las Vegas and S&M fests in Los Angeles. The most memorable spectacle for me: buxom women in kinky nurse's outfits filling volunteered male scrotal sacs with saline injected through long-nosed mean-looking needles. I swear I'm not making this up. Afterwards the submissive men would follow their mistresses' commands to display their inflated human softballs for all to see. The show caused weaklings like me to nearly faint. Not to worry, the big-balled men would gamely assure me, the swelling usually went down in just a few days.

Eventually, things between me and Hennessy changed. She started disappearing for days at a time, returning with vague excuses about "hanging out with friends." Later she filled in more detail; they were gang members for whom she claimed to be dealing drugs. I was skeptical until I began hearing whispers from the neighbors about the strange goings on while I was out. One night a series of loud knocks and shouts at the door convinced me it was true. "I have their stuff," my girlfriend explained before descending the stairs to make the banging subside.

Then there were the beatings. They began, harmlessly enough, as vicious attacks on paying submissives tied up in our garage. Not satisfied with her earnings at the club and the money she was getting from me, Hennessy, I learned, was putting in extra hours as a professional dominatrix for customers she met online. I had no problem with that as long as it didn't involve me. But then the violence started creeping inside.

Once, in a rage over something I don't recall, she threw a heavy ashtray that missed my head by an inch. It did, however, punch a hole in the wall that is still there today. Later she broke a flower vase over my skull, avoiding serious injury but drawing serious blood. Then she broke my index finger between her powerful jaws. That prompted a visit to the emergency room where, not wanting to involve police, I lied through my own clenched jaws. "This is embarrassing" I explained. "I smashed my finger in a car door."

The final straw came the night she called from the Orange County Jail. "Hi daddy," she said, "you got to bail me out." Turns out she'd been arrested for prostitution after making an unfortunate date with a team of undercover vice cops at a local hotel. "Don't worry babe," I said, "I'll be right there."

I was attending my daughter's high school graduation when the end finally came. As we walked out of the stadium, my cell phone rang. "Hey baby," she said, "where you at now?"

"Just leaving and should be home soon," I reported.

"Why don't you take Adina out for lunch?" she demurely suggested.

By the time I got home, Hennessy was gone along with miscellaneous valuables and half my clothes. The next day I had all the locks changed. But it wasn't enough to keep mayhem from entering my house.

24.

Losing Leary

It's probably just a coincidence that the demise of the *Los Angeles Times* began the night my girlfriend met the paper's editor. That said, history will record the event at which that fortuitous meeting occurred as the first time most employees heard of the imminent merger with Tribune Co., a seminal development marking the beginning of the end.

At the time, few of us fully appreciated the implications of the move. All we knew was that the Chandler family, which had made the paper great, had decided to cash in. Almost immediately we began hearing rumors about what that would mean. Tribune, we heard, was a company interested primarily in the bottom line. The most likely scenario: a major downsizing.

But the trade papers and business journals said otherwise. There would be no layoffs, they gushed, and the merger would create one of the largest media giants in the country. So we relaxed. And indeed, when the sale became final Times Mirror stock shot up 75%, amply rewarding those of us with retirement accounts.

. . .

So life in the newsroom continued as before. In fact, the past year had been one of big stories, not the least of which had been the impending end of the world. I'd been sent to cover it at the San Onofre Nuclear Generating Station in northwestern San Diego County where, as near as I could tell, my assignment was to wait for the world to end, then call in the story. The occasion was the conclusion of the twentieth century, set to occur on Dec. 31, 1999. That was the last day before the advent of something called Y2K, short for Year 2000, when prognosticators had predicted chaos due to the crash of the world's computers. The problem, they had discerned, was the rendering, in computer programs, of calendar years by only their last two digits. Hence, the argument went, in the year 2000 computers would think it was 1900 with catastrophic results including massive power failures, financial collapse, airplanes falling from the sky and, yes, nuclear power plants exploding.

So on the last day of the century, the *LA Times* dispatched reporters to conduct death watches at all major locations in Southern California likely to be flashpoints. My assignment was to spend New Year's Eve waiting to be incinerated at the San Onofre Nuclear Generating Station, one of the largest power plants in the country. At the critical moment I was standing in a glass observation booth overlooking the plant's control room when, all of a sudden, *nothing* happened! Whew, I thought, that was close. The bottom line: despite all odds, I – and every other journalist I knew – had lived to see the dawn of the new century.

Twenty-one months later another event occurred that really *did* feel like the end of the world. On September 11, 2001, I was still sleeping when my ex-wife called. "David," she shrieked into the phone, "are you watching the news? We're being attacked!!" I turned on CNN and sat in disbelief as the World Trade Center's second tower fell. Then, barely able to feel the tips of my fingers, I fumbled into my clothes and headed for work.

The newsroom was strangely quiet. About 6 p.m. an editor walked over to my desk. "We need you to work all night," he said, "in case something happens." So for the second time in a century not yet two years old, I found myself waiting for disaster.

It never came. What did come was the infernal roar of military transports flying in and out of the Joint Forces Training Base in nearby Los Alamitos; an unworldly sound on an otherwise silent night when all civilian air transport was grounded. It reminded me of the only other time I'd had any connection to the base; nearly a decade before when the paper had sent me there to monitor National Guard movements during the 1992 Los Angeles riot. Barred from entering, I was sitting in my car just outside the gate when a military police officer approach with gun drawn. "Put your hands on the dashboard," he ordered, a little shakily I thought as I quickly complied. "Who are you and what are you doing?"

By then he was standing next to me with the gun almost touching my temple through the open driver's side window. I felt like I was on a movie set, which seems to be a recurring theme with me when guns are pointed at my head. "I'm a reporter," I said, as calmly as I could, though my hands were shaking. "My ID is in the bag on the seat next to me."

He eyed it suspiciously. "Keep your left hand on the dash," he instructed, "and slowly open the bag with your other hand. No sudden moves or I'll splatter your brains all over the windshield." Apparently he was in the same movie.

Sitting in the newsroom nine years later listening to the planes rumbling overhead, I felt like I still had that gun to my head. The phones kept ringing all night; people wanted to know if we were at war. As far as I was concerned, we *were*. Only it wasn't the kind of war we expected, nor the kind we had seen before. All my previous assumptions regarding war and peace had been shaken to the core. The way forward was, at best, unclear. And so, for a time, I retreated into the past.

• • •

It began with the contemplation of caves. They are dark places to which we retire to escape the world or, in some cases, glimpse a new one. Osama Bin Laden was said to have retreated to the caves of eastern Afghanistan in the days following 9/11. It was in an underwater cave that I experienced the solitude of silt. And it was a cave in Laguna Beach to which Timothy Leary, the guru of LSD, brought his followers before being a revolutionary meant carrying a gun.

In 2003 the *Los Angeles Times* sent me there to find it, a task for which I felt uniquely qualified. I had seen Leary twice in my life: first in 1966 when my friend, Tony – the same guy who'd set me straight on Vietnam – drove a few of us to the Santa Monica Civic Auditorium where the great man was making an appearance. I remember the trip vividly because halfway there Tony told us he'd ingested some of Leary's favorite drug and was imagining the car 10 feet above the pavement and spinning in glitter as we shot down the freeway. It was the first time I felt a fear for my life that was actually *palpable*.

Leary was resplendent in garlands and white robe, sitting in a lotus position at center stage surrounded by adoring, tripping fans with long hair and beads as he narrated a light show on the screen directly behind him. We closed our eyes and let him draw us into his powerful world of cosmic relevance and fantasy. It was a sensation that would become familiar over the next half-decade: a strange twinge of anticipation and fear, a daunting quality of lightness and awe that, for me, would come to define an era.

I thought about that as I journeyed back to Leary's cave. Like many historical quests, this one began with the tale of a survivor, someone who had actually been there. Neal Purcell's claim to fame is that he's the guy who busted the famous countercultural guru and made it stick. It happened in 1968 when he was a rookie Laguna Beach police patrolman. Purcell later went on to become the city's police chief, and eventually retired as interim chief of Anderson, a small

Northern California town where I caught up with him by phone. "It was an accident," he said of the highly publicized arrest the day after Christmas. "I was out on patrol around 11 p.m. when I turned into Woodland Drive where Leary rented a house and saw a car stopped in the middle of the street."

In it were Leary, his wife, Rosemary, and their son, John. Also inside the car, mostly in Rosemary's fur bag and sewn into pouches in John's shirt, was a large quantity of marijuana and hashish, possession of which was then a felony. Though neither realized it at the time, the arrest Purcell made that night was a turning point in both their lives: the young police officer became famous and Leary became a fugitive. It was while serving a ten-year sentence stemming from the case that the "high priest of LSD," with the help of Eldridge Cleaver and others, escaped from the California Men's Colony in San Luis Obispo. He then went to Afghanistan, where he hid until 1973 when he was recaptured and extradited to California to serve out his term while his "spiritual" spouse, Joanna, took care of business.

In the late sixties, though, Leary was America's patron saint of hippies and a controversial figure who locals saw, depending on their sensibilities, as either a poetic visionary or a self-centered dope pusher preying on kids. "They'd get loaded, go up to those caves and maybe spend a couple of nights up there chanting to the moon," Purcell said.

Ah, those illusive caves. For years, the policeman told me, one was marked by a peace symbol with the guru's name etched high in a wall. Yet his description of its location was so vague that I decided to make further inquiries. A former drug dealer who claimed to have known Leary but now described himself as a devout Christian Republican told me about Mystic Arts on South Coast Highway where the local acid heads often gathered. "If you pull up the tiles you can still see the smoke stains," said Moe Riasdana, proprietor of the Nina Rug Gallery standing where Timothy Leary and his minions once passed joints cross-legged on the floor.

Then I found Kent Kelley, who had managed the place when it was what he described as the "quintessential head shop" complete with organic food, metaphysical art and the obligatory meditation room with a fireplace in back. At 55, Kelley still had shoulder length hair and now owned another place in town called Blind Faith, an "automatic eclectic emporium" boutique named after an iconic 1969 album featuring Eric Clapton and Steve Winwood. "People came from all over the world and Leary would be there every day," Kelley recalled of Mystic Arts in the 1960s. "It was one of his frequent stops. The last time I talked to him, just before he died, he mentioned the shop and how it had been the real thing."

Then he gave me a present: directions to Leary's house. Woodland Drive, I soon discovered, wasn't what it used to be. Once a ramshackle haven for renegade hippies, the place now looked clean, suburban and pricey. But a peek into a backyard seemed almost like a glance back in time: There, where the canyon basks in a convergence of greenery and sky set against a sheer cliff, it was easy to imagine an extended family of longhairs – perhaps Leary among them – lounging in the sun of a summer afternoon. I paused to savor the moment, then started knocking on doors. The third one was gold.

"A lot of people have told me that Leary lived here," said the woman, about my age, who opened it a crack. "There's definitely some trippy energy here." The aging cottage was small with gray and pink trim. I imagined flowers in its windows and paisley on its walls. "It's definitely cool that he lived here," the woman went on. "That whole era was unique; you can't coordinate what's happening today with what was going on then."

Suddenly the moment was over. She'd like to ask me in, the woman said, but she was way too busy – perhaps another time. Yes, she said, she remembers some caves; one of them had a couch in it. She told me roughly how to get there and I set out, confident that my efforts would soon be rewarded.

But finding the legendary caves of Leary proved to be a challenge. I now had several sets of instructions from people who claimed to have seen them and, though they overlapped, no two sets were the same. I drove out Laguna Canyon Road seeking a trail that supposedly started somewhere around Big Bend Drive. Not finding it, I drove to the end of a street called Canon Acres Drive to try the trail there. But that turned out to be the walkway to a long-abandoned house rambling about a hundred yards up the hill to a dead end.

If I couldn't find the caves by hiking *up*, I decided, maybe I could find them hiking *down*. So I drove to a parking lot at the top of the hill from where I could see for miles. Following yet another set of instructions, I looked for a dirt path meandering down towards the sea. But there were a myriad of them, so I arbitrarily picked one, walked a few hundred yards down, crisscrossed and retraced my steps. Finally I reached a boulder overlooking Laguna Canyon Road snaking toward the sparkling ocean beyond. There I stopped, listened, tried to feel what Leary must have felt. But all I heard was the whistling wind before walking slowly back to my car.

I saw Leary once more before his death of prostate cancer in 1996. It was probably in the late '80s, long after I'd become a drug-eschewing parent. By then he was making a living any way he could, including brief stints as a stand-up comedian. The performance at Long Beach City College was attended by a sparse crowd of erstwhile hippies like me come to see a fallen idol, and youngsters curiously regarding this quaint figure from the past.

He seemed a caricature of what he once had been. The audience was polite, but mildly embarrassed. And it dawned on me then, as it did later in Laguna Canyon, that Leary the man doesn't matter. What matters is Leary the *idea*, Leary the *myth*, Leary the figment of a generation's imagination – a link to the exuberance and foibles of our youth.

"He'll take you up, he'll bring you down, he'll plant your feet back firmly on the ground," read the lyrics of a Moody Blues song famously touting the acid guru's death long before he actually died. "He flies so high, he swoops so low, he knows exactly which way he's gonna go."

Timothy Leary illuminated a colorful moment in time, shining his own peculiar light on some of an era's stranger hues. Like those caves, his legacy is illusive. It seemed somehow right that I would never find them.

25.

Stalking the Golden Calf

And yet I had not tired of seeking icons from the past. So in 2004 I returned to Berkeley looking for the man with the golden calf. It was as if I felt compelled to revisit the scenes of my youth; as if I feared that somehow I had missed what I'd been seeking all these years and so had to go back before going forward. When I thought about it later, it seemed that in some uncanny way I sensed that my life was about to change, enter a new phase, but only if I could tie up some loose ends first. So I went back to the place where I'd spent an important part of my life and cut my teeth as a journalist. I went back looking for someone I once knew.

He called himself Zakatarious and had a very distinct world view. The earth was checkmated, he believed, because each of its inhabitants was trapped in a separate reality, thus doomed to eternal conflict over whose vision should ultimately prevail. His solution: become a pagan, worship the golden calf and usher in a new era of peace by accepting all gods, be they religious, political or ideological.

To prove his point, he planned to mount the makeshift idol on a trailer for a pilgrimage across America ending on the White House lawn where President Richard M. Nixon himself would be overcome with awe.

As far as I know, that pilgrimage never happened. At least not for me because I left Berkeley and eventually settled down, got married, had kids, built a career, acquired a mortgage and became a conservative. But I never forgot Zakatarious, never entirely abandoned the memory of infinite possibilities he once had inspired. Three decades later, moved by the energizing e-mail of a wandering daughter the same age as I had been in Berkeley, I'd come back to see if some of that old passion could be rekindled. "I went on a three-day trek through bamboo forests and yellow rice fields," Adina had written from a village in Thailand. And so I'd decided to brave the jungles of my past.

Berkeley takes a little getting used to after you've been away so long. Walking down Telegraph Avenue, my initial inclination was to tell street people to get haircuts and panhandlers to get jobs; perhaps subconsciously chastising my own younger self.

On my first day in town I met an interesting pair: brothers from Texas who said they'd run away to become professional skateboarders. "You can't skate in Texas like you can out here," the older of the two, 19, explained in earnest. Two weeks after arriving, however, he'd been grounded by a broken axle and now was begging for money to replace it. Next to him on the sidewalk, his little brother – also a wannabe professional at 12 – sat begging too. "We live in a shelter," the younger boy said. And their means of support? "Oh," he assured me, "we get money from the state."

Once I might have found this romantic. Now my first inclination was to give them a lecture on self-reliance.

Next I inadvertently wandered into a nearby protest march. Following the residual instincts of my previous life, I dumbly followed, wondering what was in store. The marchers stopped near the place I'd first seen Zakatarious, and there made their stand. They were angry, some proclaimed over a loudspeaker, at the state's temporary repeal of the bill allowing undocumented workers to get driver's licenses. Thirty years ago, I might have grabbed the microphone and proclaimed my solidarity. Today I just shook my head and sauntered on.

How had I strayed so far after leaving this town? It's not easy, looking back on a life, to pinpoint the moment that everything changed. Perhaps because there never is such a moment, just a chain of tiny decisions that alter your path. I remembered the first time I realized that I wanted a house during that long night in Guatemala when it occurred to me that I could die and no one would know what had happened or where to look. Just like that, I turned some magic corner of the soul. Getting married had seemed natural to me then. And having kids. And, eventually, finding gainful employment to support both choices.

It had been more recently, after Sept. 11, that my politics had changed. Feeling angry and vulnerable, I embraced a brand of conservatism that I once had eschewed. I was happy, though. The mortgage got paid, usually on time. I had good work, love, and weekends were free. Rarely did I think of Zakatarious. Until the day I received that email from my daughter.

"We ran into elephants in the wild and stopped at the occasional waterfall to shower," Adina wrote. "I stayed with this crazy Thai family that runs a guesthouse. They sit around drinking and showing off magic tricks to each other like making cigarettes move by themselves using static electricity, card tricks, metal puzzles, games that they've mathematically mastered to win every time, and they even taught me how to make fish out of water bottles..."

I had three reactions. The first was that it sounded like a John Irving novel. The second that she had better be careful. And the third, a longing I hadn't felt in years – for the golden calf and all it entails.

For several days in Berkeley, I didn't think any of that could be found, then I ran into Julia Vinograd. She was a woman I recalled from my own time in this Peter Pan town; the people's poet, someone who blew bubbles in your face and hawked words on the street. Now she was gray and walked with a stoop, but the Bubble Lady still blew those bubbles.

"Tell me," I asked, "do you remember a guy called Zakatarious?"

Of course, she recalled, he was one of the more memorable hecklers of the Jesus freaks. "I haven't seen the golden calf in ages," she said, "but it was an interesting idea."

An idea which, for me, had come to represent the exuberance and unfettered optimism of youth. And then I realized another thing: that the golden calf changes form. And that, despite my newfound personal conservatism, mortgage, stock options and residence in a world decidedly inhospitable to calf-worshipping pagans, a bit of the glittering animal still resided within. Only it had little to do with how I voted or where I slept or even what I did for a living. It had to do with how I felt. More specifically, what I remembered. And most important, the values I passed to my children.

I never did find Zakatarious. And the closest I ever came to learning what became of him was years later when the administrator of an online forum called to pick my brain. Some of the group's more imaginative members, he explained, had concocted the theory that the legendary Berkeley character – said to still be living in a camper somewhere in Northern California – was really the Zodiac Killer, a never-captured serial murderer who had terrorizd the Bay Area in the late 1960s and early '70s. I strongly poohpooed the idea.

Shuffling down Telegraph Avenue in 2004 on my last night in town, though, I met someone who perhaps would soon be learning the lesson I had learned long ago. "Spare Change for Bus Ticket Home?" his sign read. "On My Way to Save the World (ask me how)."

"OK," I said, "I'll take the bait."

He told me he was 25 and had left San Antonio six months before to find a solution to the world's problems here among the street people of this magic place. Now he was on his way back to share what he'd learned, but I stopped him before he could say any more. "Good luck," I offered, handing him a dollar. He smiled as only a young man can, and I knew instinctively that he would indeed make his way home. Just as everyone eventually does. Just as did the group that I would soon follow as my restless search continued.

David Haldane

26.

Head on a Stick

The ticket agent at Los Angeles International Airport was alarmingly insistent. "They'll cut off your head and put it on a stick," she said with authority. "It's not too late to cancel." Great, I thought, just what I need. Fingering the bottle of Xanax in my pocket, I sauntered off toward the gate.

It was a group of people going home, in fact, that had brought me here. They were en route to Zamboanga, a city in the southern Philippines that, since Sept. 11, had been saddled with a reputation as the breeding ground for Filipino terrorists, a rap that kept tourists away and seriously damaged the local economy.

To be completely honest, the place *did* serve as home to at least one group of Muslim extremists, some of whom occasionally got nasty. And indeed, there *had* been some kidnappings, shootings and, yes, even a beheading or two.

But why hold grudges; thousands of residents, probably even the majority, lived there relatively unscathed. And terrorism, the city's patrons wanted the world to know, was only one part of what their town was about; the other part was *street dancing*. To prove the point, a group of former Zamboanga residents in Southern California had organized a pilgrimage to the place of their birth for its annual fiesta – an event featuring lots of said dancing – and invited me along. Their message: that despite the old admonition, you actually *can* go back home and even have some fun doing it. My own analysis: probably a lot more fun than getting the *Times* to pay your fare.

Eventually, after much haggling, my employers and I struck a deal; I would cover the plane fare and they would give me some paid time "off" for the trip. In exchange, I would write a story. Several stories, in fact. It was a far cry from the old days when the paper would send anybody anywhere at a moment's notice flying first class but, hey, the so-called "Velvet Coffin" that was once the *LA Times* had long ago been buried.

• • •

Now I was sitting on an airplane in the throes of a Xanax stupor. It was in that altered state that I passed most of the nearly 15 hours it took to get to Manila. From there it was just a matter of hopping aboard a domestic flight and, voila! I would be in the renowned city of flowers.

First, though, there was another pressing task, one that would have a definite sobering effect despite the tranquilizers I had ingested. Specifically it was to check out the world's last group of unsettled Vietnamese refugees who, 30 years after the Vietnam War, still occupied small dank rooms in one of the poorest sections of Manila. Most of them had recently gotten permission to emigrate to the U.S., which is why the *Times* was interested. "I'm just happy that my family has a future," one of them, Hanh Luong, the 48-year-old mother of two young boys, told me through an interpreter. "Whatever job is offered me I will take it, even if it's washing dishes or cleaning the bathroom."

Dozens of less lucky souls, on the other hand, had been rejected for immigration and now appeared doomed to spending many more years – perhaps the rest of their lives – surviving as illegal street vendors in Manila, or worse, subsisting in barely habitable shambles on Palawan, a remote island 360 miles southwest of the city where the original Vietnamese refugee camp had been located.

Landing at the small airport there, I was greeted by a frail middle-aged Vietnamese woman who literally threw herself at my feet begging for help. I told her I would do what I could, knowing that there was absolutely nothing I could do. Later, in a village called Viet Ville where a handful of refugees still languished, I saw something I would never forget: a naked man locked in a bare cell staring at the same bleak concrete walls he'd been staring at for 20 years. "He went crazy because they ate his brother," a lone caretaker said.

The story was that in 1983 the man had escaped from Vietnam. But the boat floundered and was lost at sea for several weeks, forcing its occupants to resort to cannibalism to survive. Among those serving as nourishment was the man's younger brother, a fact that had pushed him over the edge. So now he spent his days carrying on imaginary conversations with his dead sibling and babbling to passersby through an open window about finding a good woman and moving to America.

"As long as I stay here I will take care of him," promised the caretaker, whose own immigration was blocked because he had married a Filipina.

Years later, the memory of that poor insane prisoner still haunts me.

Finally arriving in Zamboanga the following week, much more immediately evident than street dancers was the line of soldiers guarding the runway with loaded M16s. One of them escorted us from our small twin-engine plane to the even smaller passenger terminal across the tarmac. There were more armed guards at its front entrance, and even one at the Garden Orchid Hotel across the street where I'd booked a room. "May I help you, sir?" he said, appearing magically at my side a little later when I wandered to the hotel's perimeter thinking to take a walk. I changed my mind and retreated back to my room to watch CNN instead.

My impression of an armed city was heightened the next day when I conducted my first interview; with Susan Camins Sanz, a native Zamboanguena who had immigrated to San Francisco and recently returned to restore her ancestral home. It was a grand old house built in the wide-open native style reminiscent of the Spanish colonial period I'd read about in novels. The most arresting sight for me, though – aside from the rusted anti-aircraft gun still mounted in the front yard from the times when the house served as headquarters to the Japanese military occupiers – was the line of bullet holes stitching the kitchen wall. It was a reminder of the day in November, 2001, when 30 Muslim rebels had died shooting it out with police in the street nearby.

"My kids have never been here because they're too scared," said Sanz, who left the city in 1968 and hadn't returned in more than three decades. "This is my home; I sense an incredible connection. You can't let fear rule your life."

And so, trying not to let it rule mine, I went out to see some street dancing. It was beautiful. So were the women. They were everywhere, like the wildflowers so celebrated in this strange and wonderful city. The lesson for me was that, even in the midst of headline-grabbing conflict, ordinary life could go on.

On the plane back to Manila, I made a startling realization; that the women of Mindanao had made a far deeper impression on me than its armed guards. Without even thinking about it, I knew I'd be back. There was one other thing of which I was certain; that I wouldn't be needing that Xanax on the flight back to LA. The truth, in fact, was that I would never need it again.

David Haldane

27.

Filipina Heart

Two years later I'm riding on the back of a motorcycle with a woman's long black hair streaming across my face. On one side is a coconut-tree forest and on the other, a jade-colored sea. As my fingers dig lightly into the firm flesh of her narrow waist, I am seized by an overwhelming certainty; that life simply doesn't get any better than this. And just like that I know I'm in love.

How does one slide from a familiar existence into another so radically different? For me, it was a matter of slipping back into something with which I was intimately familiar and had used before; classified advertising. Only it wasn't called that any more. And the technology had significantly improved since the days I'd used it to meet my first wife. Now it was not just newsprint on paper, but actual images on a screen. And instead of just wondering what a prospect was like, I could actually see her and hear her face-to-face in *real* time!

The web site was called *Filipinaheart.com* and, like so many things in life, it had come to me on a whim. Back from Zamboanga, I realized that I had liked what I'd seen. The women of the Philippines, I couldn't help but notice, had a strong appeal. They were beautiful, to be sure. But that wasn't all; there was also a sweetness and sincerity that, it now occurred to me, I hadn't felt from an American woman in quite some time. How could that be, I wondered? Surely sincerity is not a national trait that Filipinos have and American's lack. And then it occurred to me that what I was really sensing was far more personal and subjective; a frank, unabashed and, yes, sincere interest in *me*.

Perhaps the problem was mine alone; maybe I simply wasn't worthy of serious attention from any female save one hoping to escape from a developing country. I had to accept the possibility that that was true. The more I thought about it, though, the less sense that made. While I certainly wasn't Robert Redford, neither was I an extra from *The Walking Dead*. And while I certainly wasn't rich and famous, I at least had regular employment that was both interesting and gainful.

So why had I encountered such disappointing responses from American women? Part of it, I had to admit, lay in my odd dating choices; a 19-year-old bipolar black stripper, after all, wasn't exactly the perfect candidate for a potential life partner for a 50-something man. But why was I choosing women like that? And what about the others, women closer to my age with seemingly compatible lifestyles and resumes? Why had I found it so difficult to find a mate? I certainly hadn't wanted for dates; lots of women were willing to go out and have fun. Yet there always seemed to be a kind of distance to it, a way of keeping everything at arm's length.

Even when these women were willing to make commitments, it seemed, there were major gaps. They were almost intangible, more of a vague sense than anything concrete, but absolutely present nonetheless; the feeling that I needed them more than they needed me, a subtle perception, in fact, that they didn't really *need* me at all. Certainly they tolerated me, perhaps even enjoyed being with me, but actually *needed* me – I didn't think so. Was this the result of years of feminism, the often repeated mantra that women are complete unto themselves and that needing a man is a sign of weakness? The idea that, to achieve equality, women had to stop being women and be more like men? Or had these women, many of them quite wonderful, been so badly burned in the past that their baggage was too heavy to allow for any sort of profound love or trust?

Whatever it was, I sensed a real difference in the Filipinas I encountered, and it had nothing to do with submissiveness. The Philippines, after all, had a long history and culture of strong women; two of the country's presidents – including one of the most beloved – have, in fact, been women. A recent survey conducted by the International Labor Organization and reported by the *Washington Post* ranks the Philippines fourth in the world – well above the United States – in the percentage of management positions in the country, just under 47%, held by women. And yet the culture also embraced traditional values in matters of marriage and family. These women, though strong, still inhabited a universe in which men occupied an important and unambiguous place.

And so, sensing all of this rather than really knowing it, I googled "women in the Philippines" one night, and up popped *Filipinaheart.com*. It started out as a lark; I began spending evenings on the web site chatting with women for fun. Some were obviously looking for handouts; after being taken in by one who said she needed money for her college tuition, I quickly learned to ignore anyone mentioning sick relatives or unpaid hospital bills in the first five minutes of any conversation.

Some were obviously manufacturing fake biographies, posting pictures of models or actresses instead of their own. One "woman" turned out to be a man. Most, however, seemed like decent folk being honest about what they were seeking. And what many were seeking, amazingly, was someone like *me*. It was as if I had been magically transformed from an invisible older man into a rock star whose company women craved. Of course that appealed to my ego. On a deeper level, though, it spoke to my need to be needed. These were women who, for the most part, wanted what people have *always* wanted: marriage, family, security and a loving home. And the longer I talked to them, the more I realized that those were things I wanted, too.

Over the next several months, my search gradually narrowed. One night, glancing at a chat box on my screen, I saw the image of a beautiful black-haired dark-eyed young woman resting her head on a desk in what looked like an Internet cafe. What got my attention was that she wasn't trying to get mine. And so our conversation began.

• • •

The thing that impressed me about Ivy right off were her detailed responses to the questions I posed. We discovered very quickly that we had lots in common, including similar dreams and outlook on life. More importantly, though, we wanted the same things that we valued in the same way. "I'm looking for someone who will stay with me for the rest of my life," I confessed in an email barely two weeks into our talk. The next day came her reply. "David, we have to realize that love is not enough to make a relationship work; we need trust, respect, time, effort and total commitment...I believe you can fall in love *after* you marry because ... we should not let *passion* but *wisdom* decide."

She seemed wise beyond her years. And yet I wondered what people would say, especially regarding the considerable difference – more than three decades – in our ages. I raised the issue with Ivy on several occasions. "You say that I am young," she responded, "but I am fixed in my mind and know what I want. Don't worry about the age gap because it doesn't matter; most important is that I meet a real person who can be trusted and loved."

At times I wondered whether I was just being played. But as the discourse continued, her message remained consistent. And so I decided to go and find out.

28.

Karma

Before departing, though, I need to write a chapter that I didn't intend to write; *this* one. It is notably absent, in fact, from earlier drafts of this book. The reason is that it doesn't contribute to the simple narrative I planned to tell: boy experiences American women, becomes disillusioned, goes for a Filipina and lives happily ever after. In fact, it detracts considerably from that narrative. But the omission kept tugging at me, and I finally realized why: the excluded material lays out another *karmic* narrative that is larger and far more profound. So here it is: Ivy was not my first Filipino wife. No, that dubious distinction belongs to a woman named Anna - from where else but Zamboanga.

We met in the usual way: on *Filipinaheart.com*. And the first time I saw her, I was smitten like a kitten. I will spare you the details of our long-distance courtship and engagement. Let's just say that the parade of red flags I missed began on the day her parents took us to get our marriage license at Zamboanga City Hall. "Tell me," Anna's mom asked, "of all the girls in the Philippines, whatever made you pick this one?"

Though I was too offended to realize it at the time, her question had very little to do with my intended's desirability, which was quite ample, and everything to do with the fact that she was already an unwed mother with a two-year-old child, a status that in a Catholic country, at least back then, still carried a modicum of shame.

Nazis and Nudists

After the wedding – a fairly ostentatious affair held at one of the city's leading churches followed by a reception at its most prestigious hotel – we separated for the usual immigration process, which took almost a year. Then one day, boom, it was over and she was here.

I still remember my new wife's first days in America. At the all-night diner where we stopped on the way home from the airport, she grinned and commented that she'd never been served by white people before. The first time she used the garbage disposer, she wanted to know where all the garbage went. I had to show her how to turn on the water for a bath while she marveled that there was actually a *carpet* on the bathroom floor. And during a walk at a nearby nature center, she saw her first squirrel which she said she recognized from cartoons.

There were other notable firsts as well: the solo walk during which she was afraid to cross a street that was so wide, the dip in a public swimming pool where she insisted on wearing clothes, and a memorable encounter with cream cheese which, after spreading it on her hot dog and bacon, she declared delicious.

Meanwhile the red-flag parade continued completely invisible to my love-splattered eyes. The first sign I missed was probably her choice of employment: a downtown karaoke bar frequented by Filipino seamen berthed at the Port of Long Beach. Anna worked graveyard as a waitress/singer/entertainer. I should have realized something was amiss the first time I picked her up at 3 a.m. and our ride home was interrupted by the ring of her cell phone.

"Who the hell was that?" I asked after she'd hung up,

"Oh, just one of my customers," my wife demurely explained.

Astounded at the apparent naiveté of this young new immigrant, I delivered a stern fatherly lecture on the perils of so generously sharing her number. She listened intently, promised never to do it again and then, I'm sure, took it underground. Later, after she'd moved on to a career at a gambling casino, one of my friends commented on Anna's propensity for getting dolled up before work. Oh that's so sweet, I thought; she wants to look good for her husband. Who was being naïve now?

Finally there was the weekend she was invited to a coworker's wedding. Great, I said, that should be lots of fun. Well, uh, she said, looking at me like I was an alien, but only *she* was invited. Don't you think it a little strange, I suggested, that a married woman would be invited to a wedding without her spouse? In the end, she decided to stay home rather than take me along.

. . .

It was about then that I started noticing the secretive calls. Her phone would ring and she'd furtively take it to another room. Or, finding that impossible, quickly promise to call back. One night, wondering why she was late, I found her outside in her parked car talking intensely on her mobile phone. It was Anna's young daughter who finally broke the bad news. By then she was 5 and I loved her like my own.

"Daddy," the little girl said whispering in my ear, "when you're at work mommy and I go see a *man*."

To her credit, Anna never denied it, though getting the full truth out of her took some time. And that truth was that she had fallen in love with a coworker at the casino with whom she'd been carrying on for months. I was devastated, but not completely undone. The marriage meant enough to me, I told her, that I was willing to try and forgive on one condition: that she give up this man. Anna agreed, and for about a week it looked like our union would be saved. Then she saw him again, called off the deal and – after three years of marriage and two of cohabitation – moved out the next day.

I have only spotty recollections of what happened next. I recall walking the sidewalks at night feeling like throwing myself in front of a bus. I also remember calling a suicide prevention hotline for the first and only time in my life. Then one day it occurred to me that I was reaping what I'd sewn. This was karma: what Anna had done to me I had done to my first wife, Dawn.

I have never been a deeply religious person. Yet I have always felt the existence, seen or unseen, of a certain balance in the world, a certain kind of justice. It is not easy to see yourself at the receiving end of that justice, especially in the midst of pain the likes of which you have never experienced. But in time, as its intensity gradually diminishes to that of an enduring ache, it is sometimes possible to put the pain in its proper perspective.

Once I had violated my marriage vows, put someone I had loved and promised to protect through the kind of agony that, at the time, I could only imagine. Now I was not just imaging but *experiencing* it; somehow that was as it should be.

Then came the next level of understanding; the more I thought about it, the more I began to see Anna as a *deliverer* rather than a tormentor. On the most obvious level, I came to understand that she had not consciously deceived me, at least not in the earliest days of our courtship and marriage. She was a young woman in need of her own kind of deliverance, and at just the right moment I had appeared as her deliverer. If she had been too quick to convince herself that she was ready to make a lifelong commitment, well, perhaps it could be forgiven.

On a deeper and more cosmic level, in fact, I began to understand that we were *each other's* deliverers. I had delivered her from a life without potential, and she ultimately delivered me from a karmic debt that I had carried for years. Indeed, it had been a cumbersome one: a debt, I came to believe, that had prevented me from moving on, prevented my life from unfolding with the natural ebb and flow in which lives are meant to unfold.

All this became exquisitely clear to me after I met Ivy. And so today I thank my first Filipino wife who, by balancing the scales, cleared a path for me to reach the woman who would change my life.

29.

Pig-on-a-Spit

That change began one day when I found myself sprinting through a rice paddy with a pregnant caribou in hot pursuit. Though ostensibly possessed of some dignity, I seemed to have lost it at least for the moment. "*Mooooooo!*" the animal moaned, obviously experiencing a measure of discomfort from her bloated condition. But never mind, I had almost reached the safety of the coconut trees beyond. My last cogent thought before getting there: that this was decidedly *not* the kind of female companionship I was seeking.

If you were to put a map of the Philippines on the wall and throw darts at it, the chances of one sticking anywhere near Caridad would be miniscule. That is, of course, unless you happened to be an expert dart thrower and knew exactly where it is, which few people – even in the Philippines – ever do. Like them, I had never heard of the thatched-hut village on Siargao Island. In fact, I had never heard of Siargao, a remote tear-shaped spot of land comprising about 170 square miles off the northeastern coast of Mindanao. So I had some serious travel planning to do.

Here's how it shook out: a 16-hour plane ride to Manila (sans Xanax), followed by a shorter flight to Cebu, then an overnight ferry trip to a medium-sized port city where Ivy met me with a cousin in tow. Before exchanging even a dozen words, the three of us had boarded a boat laden with pigs and bananas for the three-hour trip to the island.

Nazis and Nudists

I can't honestly say that it was love at first sight. The truth is that Ivy, so effusive in her emails, was too shy in person to even look me in the eye. Her cousin graciously took up the slack during awkward lulls in patter. But as we approached the pristine shore of the beautiful place where she was born, the look of the world began to change.

The first thing I noticed about Caridad, one of several rural villages on the island and home to about 1,800 souls, was its multitude of brown-skinned bright-eyed children with smiles as wide as the sky. They were everywhere, darting among stray goats and water-buffalo-drawn carts. Nobody seemed overly concerned with where each child belonged. When they were hungry, they knocked on a door and got fed; it was as simple as that. Several, in fact, were doing just that at Ivy's house as we arrived. "So..." her mother inquired in halting English as soon as she'd shown me my seat, "you want to marry my daughter."

The truth was that we hadn't yet discussed any such plans. Ivy shot me a dark-eyed apologetic glance. "Well," I responded, not wanting to be disagreeable, "what would you think of such a thing?" That was when I noticed the gathering crowd outside, already perhaps 30 people of all ages and genders grinning at me through open windows and doors. "What are *they* doing here?" I whispered to Ivy, not sure what to think. I wasn't prepared for her answer. "They've never seen a white man before," she said. So there I was: a veritable Christopher Columbus at his own private Plymouth Rock.

· · ·

The rest of the conversation passed in a whirl: What were my goals? Where did I live? Who were my relatives? What did they do? And finally, my favorite: what had gone wrong in my first marriage – the only one I'd disclosed to my potential mother-in-law – that would be fixed this time around?

Through it all, Ivy sat by me – a strong but silent presence – occasionally glancing but never touching. The questions, all from a stern mom and smiling dad with several relatives and half the village looking on, were merciless. As much as they made me squirm, though, they also commanded respect; here was a family that took seriously the admonition to protect its own.

I must have passed muster because eventually my sweetie, referred to locally as "black beauty" due to her lovely dark skin, was allowed to accompany me alone on a stroll. That's when we encountered the second round of inquisition; this one from a large group of smiling locals gathered on the beach with a teacher translating their many concerns. Obviously, the town was not inclined to let one of its favorite daughters – or *any* of its daughters for that matter – be whisked away by just anyone with a nice smile and ghostly white skin.

The next morning, safely ensconced in a small bedroom with Ivy and her two sisters on the bed and Dad, Mom, me and a brother on the floor, I was awakened at six by a bloodcurdling scream. Oh God, I thought, the Muslim rebels have come to kill us all. In fact, it was the dying cry of one of her father's pigs giving its last full measure of devotion for some crazy visiting foreigner – namely *me*. Completely acting the part, I spent the rest of the morning photographing the poor animal being roasted while Ivy explained to her relatives why her boyfriend was so interested in a pig slowly spinning on a spit. And that afternoon the family, along with the majority of its neighbors, enjoyed a festive feast of *lechon* traditionally offered on only the most special of occasions. The pig looked like the guest of honor, laid out whole on the table in all its crispy brown glory for everyone to admire and consume. The only thing missing was the apple in its mouth.

It was then that Ivy's father made what seemed like an innocent suggestion. "David," he said. "I want to show you my caribou."

Let me pause here for a word on the importance of these animals in Southeast Asia. A normally placid type of water buffalo, the caribou is literally the economic backbone of agrarian cultures like those in the rural Philippines. Weighing up to 2,000 pounds, it is the beast of choice for pulling plows, hauling carts and, yes, sometimes even eating at weddings. So it was not insignificant that Ivy's father, a rice and coconut farmer, wanted to show me his. What I didn't yet know was that these horned animals can sometimes be mean.

"OK," I gamely said, "let's go take a look."

I'm sure you can fill in the blanks. No one knows exactly what makes a caribou attack. It could be hunger, thirst or, perhaps, overwork. On the other hand, some have suggested, the animal may simply have not liked my looks or smell. Whatever its inspiration, the enormous buffalo sized me up and immediately mounted a charge.

In the annals of Caridad history, there are doubtless a handful of memorable scenes. There's the time two farmers got into a knife fight ending with one of them dead. A woman with visions others couldn't see once roamed the beaches stark naked. And there is the picture – engraved, I'm sure, in the memories of all who saw it – of the pale-faced foreigner running for his life with hat in hands.

To this day, I'm not sure how I outran that beast of burden. I suspect that the animal's pregnant condition greatly increased my chances for survival. What I *am* sure of is that, somewhere in the back of an otherwise panicked mind, I could hear the clearly discernable laughter from a crowd of delighted observers obviously enjoying their first encounter with a white man. It was time to get out of town.

30.

A Heart in the Ceiling

And so we progressed to the motorcycle by the sea. As I sat astride it with Ivy's long black mane caressing my face, a radical thought popped into my head. Gently leaning forward, I whispered it into her ear. "This is as good as it gets," I heard myself say, "I really believe that this is it." Thus began our island dream.

It's possible of course that I didn't actually utter that thought at all, but just *thought* it and then *thought* I'd uttered it. In truth it doesn't matter, because somehow the idea was born. For this was not the end but the beginning of our discussions regarding the future. Later, on a stretch of white sand once owned by her grandfather, we built a crude wooden shelter with a heart carved into its ceiling to commemorate the day. And finally, at the end of a long pier called Cloud Nine, I asked Ivy to be my wife.

For now, though, we were en route to a town called General Luna to see a man about a boat that would take us to a fair. It was no ordinary fair, mind you, but the annual fiesta in the village that, among its many claims of distinction, was the birthplace of the woman with that amazing head of hair. Ivy and I had left the charms of Caridad behind not too long before. Now we were going back, in my case bravely, in the hopes of seeing more. Though we could easily make it on wheels, she had convinced me that it would be better by sea. Arriving in General Luna half an hour later, I wasn't so sure.

The town, known to foreigners mainly as a surfing Mecca, has a history with a few dark streaks. Legend has it that the man who introduced the sport here in the early 1980s – a Hawaiian who locals referred to as "Mad Max" – died alone in his hut after a 44-day fast. I've heard one account, though, claiming that he was actually murdered for a stack of U.S. bills he kept hidden under his mat. So as Ivy negotiated with a boatman on the beach in a language I didn't understand, I was acutely aware of what I took to be the unnatural eagerness of his grin.

Then I realized that the smile had been misconstrued. We handed the stranger a thousand pesos – about $23 – to ferry us home. And, magically, as the sand receded into the distance so did my disquiet. This is my favorite part of Siargao; the skip-along-the-water, spray-in-your-face kind of feeling you get when you're, well, skipping along the water with spray in your face. It took me back to another time years before when I'd skipped along the coast of a different island, that one in Greece, thinking about how time is like a rubber band. Now, I realized, I was at the other end of that band, the place to which it had pulled me. With the possible exception of that earlier ride, this one was the most exhilarating thing I had ever experienced. And, as on that ride, it made me think about staying forever.

By then I had learned that, despite my startled reaction to the dying squeals of a pig beneath my window, this region of Mindanao, unlike some others, was not particularly prone to Muslim attacks. But even if it were, I thought – perhaps naively – I would not be able to resist its charms any more than I could resist the charms of the woman beside me.

• • •

About 45 minutes into the voyage, we passed a gorgeous white-sand beach on our left. This was Magpupungko, a Visayan word meaning "squatting rock" in deference to the boulder there that appears to balance lightly on the water in defiance of both gravity and nature. The pristine beach is famous for its natural jade-green pools, deep enough to swim in at low tide. It also, happily, is the site of nearly two acres of beachside coco land owned by Ivy's family where we would later carve that heart.

Fifteen minutes after passing Magpupungko, we tied up at Caridad beach where, traversing the sand to the little town above, we were followed by a horde of sunbaked children with broad smiles that could set the heavens ablaze.

"Hello," said a little boy, obviously proud of his patchy English. "You like it here?"

That's when it hit me: I had seen this smile before, not only on the boatman's face this morning but earlier and closer to home. It was the same inscrutable look that often graced the woman I had come to love, as mysterious to me now as on the day we met. Though I didn't know it yet, I would one day see it again on her face and others aboard a boat with two holes. And suddenly I was seized by something else I never expected: a fierce and irrational affection for the people from whom she arose.

Friends ask how I spend my time in this remote place populated by farmers and fishermen. I give them the usual answers: scuba diving, surfing, exploring towns and waterfalls and – my favorite – hopping amongst hundreds of nearby islands, some the size of your yard. To those activities I now add another: spending a fair amount of time hanging out with locals searching for the source of their smiles.

Later, walking arm-in-arm on the beach with Ivy, we came across a scene right out of my dreams. It was a hammock strung casually in the shade between coconut trees over a patchwork of grass and sand. A few paces beyond lay the crystalline sea and, beyond that, two distant islands just begging to be touched.

With a wave of her arm, my sweet companion motioned me to rest. For a moment I was seriously torn, then resisted the temptation and snapped pictures instead. For there was something I instinctively knew: if I lay down then, I might never leave. And staying was a privilege that had yet to be earned.

I began earning it a few weeks later on an island called Suyangan. If you were a bird flying over that particular land mass and happened to look down on the day I was there, you would have seen the body of the white man lying prone on the beach. That body, in fact, was my own. For most of its life it has been pampered with good food, regular tooth brushing and, until recently, relative restraint regarding the liquid nourishment it was allowed to imbibe.

But that was before I drank my first glass of *tuba*. Don't get me wrong; I am not now, nor have I ever been, an alcoholic. And, indeed, there are several other figures lying next to mine on the sand including one belonging to my future father-in-law. In fact, it is because of him that I am here, for there is one more test I must pass before becoming a part of this family.

• • •

I first got wind of it on Siargao Island, known for many wonderful things including, as I have said, its awesome surfing, large mangrove forests and gorgeous white-sand beaches. All of which pales, however, in comparison to its prodigious production of the world's best coconut wine, known locally as *too-bah*.

Let me pause here for a deep breath and short discourse on this home-brewed cultural icon with such powerful effects. The stuff comes from coconut trees. More specifically, from premature fruit stalks accessed by fearless coco-tree-climbing specialists. Over the years the sweet-tasting coco sap has become the center of a male bonding ritual in these parts; while men drink it loudly and publicly, women – if they indulge at all – typically do so in private. The drama is made all the more poignant by the fact that the elixir can be obtained only from its maker, not commercially, and turns to vinegar in days. This usually means that you go to the tree-climber's kitchen where the stuff is stored in a vat, present your own container – perhaps a Pepsi bottle – and watch it filled with this nectar of the gods. The cost in Siargao is the equivalent of about $1 for five liters, which means that you can drink a whole lot. And if the source is a relative, you can usually get it for free which means you can drink even more.

So when the father of my bride-to-be offered me a taste of his cousin's best tuba, well, it wasn't an invitation I could refuse. "*You* love my daughter," he declared tearfully, throwing a hairy arm around me in one of the few English sentences I'd ever heard him utter, "*I* love my daughter. Come, let us go!" I just hoped that the adventure would turn out better than my encounter with his caribou.

Where we ended up was aboard a borrowed pamboat for the two-hour ride to Suyangan, a neighboring island with its own spritely coconut trees and ample share of sand. It was there, around 10 a.m. at his persistent urging, that I first tasted the Creator's own sweet island drink. Let me just say that it certainly possesses some creative qualities, especially when it comes to the eyes. We're not just talking double vision here; think deep impenetrable blackness pierced by occasional splashes of pink. The thing that impressed me most, though, was how quickly it sneaks up on you. One minute you're sitting there nodding amiably with Dad, and the next...well...you're snoring deeply into the sand. Now, hours later, I've awakened on the beach only vaguely aware of where – or *who* – I am.

Few of my new buddies can help. The only language we share, after all, is the word for a sweet milky liquid prone to rapid decomposition and I'm not about to say that one again. Eventually my fiancé's dad guides me shakily back to the boat. And that's when the full precariousness of my situation becomes brutally clear; he cranks up the motor, starts out to sea, hands me the tiller and promptly passes out on deck. "Hey," I protest, but it's already too late. He groggily waves an arm – the same one that had earlier crossed my shoulder in fatherly affection – pointing generally towards the north, and that's all the help I can get!!!

Anyone who's ever operated a pamboat will tell you that it's no easy task. Especially when you're doing it for the first time in the middle of a strange ocean heading for an island you can't even see. Consisting of a narrow canoe-like hull with bamboo pontoons on each side, this primitive boat – completely devoid of instruments – runs mainly on its skipper's instincts.

And it's amazing how quickly those instincts kick in. Sitting in the middle of the Philippine Sea, I focussed every bit of my tuba-addled brain on keeping the sinking sun on my left as Dad mumbled unintelligible encouragement at my feet. If one were to draw an aerial map of our gradual course toward home that day, I'm sure it would feature lots of lazy looping swirls; perhaps enough to make the drawing saleable as a piece of modern art. And I can't even begin to describe my emotional turmoil at the prospect of losing my future wife's father at sea.

Somehow, though, the hours creep by. The afternoon wears on. Then suddenly, just before sunset, I see another horizon filled with sand. "You guys were gone a long time," says my fiancé, waiting impatiently on the beach.

"It's complicated," I tell her.

Then my soon-to-be father-in-law chimes in with a variation of his now-familiar theme. "We *both* love my daughter," he says, still groggy from the ride.

And so it is that I, a mere foreigner challenged by a severe headache and fair degree of cluelessness, am able to pass the infamous test of tuba. I am not a stranger anymore; I have advanced to the bosom of the family. Thus the stage is set. Time to bring my sweet unvarnished love to the fires of the kiln that is America.

David Haldane

31.

My Imported Bride

Had we been in more of a hurry, Ivy's first day in America might also have been her last. As it was, she got her initial glimpse of home from the cab of a tow truck. The accident happened 15 minutes after my sorely missed fiancé, who I'd left in the Philippines for the processing of her visa, strolled down the welcome ramp at Los Angeles International Airport. A photograph taken in the airport lobby that night tells it all; the two of us, arm in arm, with her clutching a bouquet of roses and both of us sporting grins stretching all the way to Manila.

For me, at least, the grin never narrowed. That's why, driving through the tunnel towards Long Beach, I didn't notice the car in front of us stopping. Frankly it was because my eyes were diverted by a friendlier sight: the lovely young woman in the passenger's seat beside me. The collision was jarring; a sickening crunch as the horn let loose a wail and both airbags deployed throwing bursts of hissing steam in our faces. We jumped out of the car expecting it to immediately explode. It didn't. Instead, the driver of the vehicle in front jumped out too and started cursing at me in Spanish.

My little Mazda, we eventually learned, was totaled. And though there seemed to be no injuries at the time, the insurance company ended up paying thousands to a family claiming that their backs were in pain. The main damage, though, was to my pride. And, indeed, many months later Ivy confessed that, after her first freeway ride nearly ended in death, she seriously considered hopping onto the next plane for home. To my eternal gratitude, that never happened. "I just didn't tell my mom," she one day explained.

Our travails, however, were far from over: some time later we were at our Los Alamitos house in northern Orange County, California, pouring drinks for our guests when the police arrived. It was 3 p.m. on a Saturday, and we were hosting a friend's baby shower, complete with *lechon*, in our open garage. The two officers surveyed the scene carefully before striding toward me with bad news. "We got a complaint from your neighbor," one of them said with a nod. After they sorted it out and determined that we weren't committing any crimes or posing a public nuisance, I approached the neighbor in question. She was a woman in her 60s who had lived in this quiet town home complex for many years. And she wasn't accustomed to seeing garage parties here featuring dark-skinned people eating pigs on a spit.

"Your personal life is so messed up," she coolly informed me.

"Well thanks," I responded, "we appreciate your understanding."

What she didn't understand at all was that these pig-eating fests were essential to our well-being. They had started months before as an antidote to Ivy's loneliness. Eight weeks after her dramatic arrival, we'd been married at an intimate ceremony in a small chapel near Las Vegas. When the honeymoon was over and the hoopla spent, however, there was this to contend with: the profound silence of our lives.

I vividly remember my wife's first impressions. She too had never seen streets so wide which, for a time, were too intimidating to cross. Operating a washing machine and microwave were skills she had to acquire. And, accustomed to the continuous sounds of crowing roosters, barking dogs and squealing children, her most difficult adjustment was to the pervasive emptiness surrounding our house.

"It's as if we have no neighbors," Ivy often complained.

We filled that void with friends much like us. In the absence of the large family and community structures of the Philippines, we created a substitute family here in the wilderness of America. Consisting mostly of American men with Filipino wives and, increasingly, the children they produced, our group – which began when some of the women connected online – evolved into an active, though informal, association with frequent gatherings at various homes. Like any family, this one had its share of squabbles. But it also formed the core of our social life, functioning much like Ivy's village back home. Within this circle we celebrated holidays, baptisms, birthdays and baby showers. When one woman got pregnant, the others brought her food. And on the rare occasions that tragedy struck, we grieved together as one.

To be honest, it reminded me of my childhood. For my mother too had been an immigrant. And, like Ivy, she had surrounded herself with friends from the old country. Hardly a Sunday passed without a gathering in someone's backyard, little parties we called *kaffe klatches*. Instead of roasted pig, the menu featured strudel. And, much as in our get-togethers more than half a century later, the women chattered in their native tongue while the men hovered nearby and children played tag on the grass. I have lifelong friendships that began with those long-ago games of tag.

There was another similarity too; like those immigrant German Jews, we were often misunderstood by our peers, a fact driven home on the day we went public. It all started during lunch with an editor I'd worked for at the *Times* now employed by *Orange Coast* magazine. "So tell me what you been up to," he said, "fill me in on the last eight years."

As I did his eyes grew large. "Are you telling me that you married a younger woman from the Philippines who you met online?" he asked incredulously. "How would you feel about writing on that?" And so we were off. When the 3,000-word essay appeared in the magazine's

April, 2012, issue under the title of "My Imported Bride," my ears started imploding. By early the next morning, it was clear that we had a hit. A hit, that is, if you define such as creating a buzz. But buzzes aren't always good to hear and this one, frankly, sounded like it was coming from a chainsaw.

The onslaught began with a call from a friend indicating that publication of my story was the lead item in that day's *LA Observed*, the most widely read media blog in Los Angeles. Within hours I'd been asked to do a reading for a popular news show on the local California Public Radio station. And from there everything mushroomed; my 15 minutes of infamy had clearly begun. But it was the story in the *Orange County Weekly*, an alternative newspaper not unlike the one I'd worked for years before, that elicited the most interesting – and, I must say, *chilling* – response. "If I were him I'd sleep with one eye open," a reader wrote after perusing the article entitled "David Haldane Has a Mail-Order Bride and Wants His OC Neighbors to be Cool with it." Why? Because, the reader continued, "His new little honey may not think this 'arrangement' is so wonderful."

Over the next few days the critiques flew in, not only on the original magazine's website but on those of a host of other publications and blogs that had picked up the story. "Wow so sad," someone wrote. "She married him for the US, and all he wants is a trophy wife and hot sex." Commented another: "All I can say is Oh My God, he looks like her GRANDFATHER!! I wouldn't let that shriveled thing near me for any amount of money."

Gradually a common theme began to emerge: that I was a loser who, unable to attract a woman in the "normal" way, had resorted to preying on vulnerable young females in a developing country. Not only was I exploiting Ivy, the rap continued, but, by extoling the process, providing aid and comfort to human trafficking worldwide.

And, finally, I was a male chauvinist pig capable of happiness only with a weak woman who subordinates her own needs to his. "The key in this story," one reader commented, "is 'traditional values' which is barely disguised code for accepting a subservient position in marriage."

Then a few supportive voices emerged. "Who are any of you to judge the happiness or motivation of two people you don't know?" a reader wondered. "Relationships are hard and it's great if two people can make it work."

And finally there was this, responding directly to the charge of "traditional values" as subservience: "Or it could, you know, mean *traditional values*. Someone who still…values the sanctity of marriage…Someone who believes that crass materialism will never equate to the value of a family…Someone who believes that children are a blessing and not just a fashion accessory or tool with which to manipulate your spouse. All of which are sorely lacking in the bulk of 'modern' American women."

That one almost made me cry; I couldn't have said it better myself.

Through it all, Ivy maintained an attitude of stoicism; after reading a few letters, she simply stopped. "Do any of these people know us?" she asked rhetorically responding to my expressions of concern. "Do they have our address, will they come to our door?" Then why, she wondered, should she deign to be bothered?

I, on the other hand, read every word and felt chastened. But I also felt something else: surprise and disappointment at the ferocity of the assault. For ours, in theory, is a tolerant and open society, is it not? I couldn't imagine anyone publically expressing this kind of outrage – at least not to a supposedly liberal audience like KPPC's or the *Orange County Weekly's* – regarding, say, a same-sex relationship or one between black and white. Yet Ivy and I, it seemed, were fair game; obviously there were some major gaps in the texture of our tolerance.

"It's funny," one man wrote, "that these losers never want to settle in their bride's home country. If they love, love, love these folks so bad, why don't they live where they can be surrounded by them – really take in the culture, both good and bad?"

It was hard to argue with that. The time would come, in fact, when I wouldn't argue at all.

David Haldane

32.

The End Times

One summer night a *Los Angeles Times* reporter died at his desk. It happened so quietly that the security guard on duty thought he was taking a nap. So did I. "Carry on," the guard had said, winking at me as he passed to continue his rounds.

By then I was working nights at the *Times*' Orange County bureau in Costa Mesa. The reporter in question, a sports stringer in his mid-40s, had apparently come to the newsroom to report some late scores. When the guard saw him at 10 p.m. the man's head was resting comfortably on his desk with the small TV above it flashing sports news. Four hours later he was in exactly the same position and the news was long over. The guard tried to wake him up. Then called 911. Paramedics later told us that the reporter, with whom I had only a nodding acquaintance, had experienced a massive heart attack sometime during the early evening hours.

For me it was a wakeup call, not unlike the one delivered unsuccessfully that night by the security guard to the unfortunate corpse. Unlike him, however, I still had enough life left in me to receive it loud and clear. For years, or at least the last several of them, I'd been jokingly telling people that I had no plans to retire. Instead, I'd say, I would keep working until I died at my desk and got carried out feet first. Now a fellow reporter with a desk not far from mine had done just that. The moment was sobering; was this really how I wanted to spend the rest of my life?

For better or worse, I never had to answer that question because very soon it was answered *for* me. It happened on a Monday in July. For weeks we'd been hearing rumors of layoffs, but by then that was not uncommon and the reductions, when they did occur, were never as deep or as bad as the rumors predicted.

So, reporting for work at the usual time, I was not feeling particularly stressed. But the editor approached me before I sat down. "Take a walk with me," he suggested, putting a brotherly arm on my shoulder. As we walked slowly down the hall, he started to talk. "As you know," he said, "these are very difficult times at the paper; today began with the publisher getting fired."

That was certainly interesting news, but I didn't get where this was headed. Then I saw where we *both* were headed: to the human resources office in the lobby. "David," my editor said, "it pains me to tell you that we're letting you go." Suddenly a casual stroll down the hall became a walk of death; I was an inmate and he was the warden leading me to execution. I could almost envision a rosary-fingering priest walking ahead of us chanting in Latin. And the people who moments before had been colleagues now seemed like fellow inmates banging spoons against their bars.

"How long have you known about this?" I asked my soon-to-be-former boss.

"Not long," he said with a sigh, "only since this morning."

I don't remember much of what happened after that; they made me sign some papers and enroll in a course for career counseling. I noticed a box of tissues on the HR manager's desk, but never deigned to use them. Then it was all over and the editor was walking me back to the newsroom. "You can leave if you want," he said, "or stick around to say goodbye."

By the end of the shift my electronic key card had been deactivated and there was blood all over the floor. In what was later described as one of the deepest cuts by a major U.S. newspaper in recent history,

250 *Times* staffers – more than half of them writers and editors – were shown the door that day. It amounted to a 17 percent reduction in editorial staff - the first in a long series of layoffs that have never stopped.

My final *Los Angeles Times* byline had appeared the day before, a Sunday, over a story about 8,000 people baring their asses to passing trains in Orange County. "It's so liberating that it's contagious," explained one participant in the 29th annual "train mooning" festival along the tracks in Laguna Niguel. "I just can't stop."

After 23 years as a *Times* staff writer, I was back on the tracks myself. Part of me wished it had happened a week earlier so that I too could have mooned a few trains. Two months later, Lehman Brothers – the fourth largest investment bank in the United States – declared bankruptcy and the stock market crashed. America's worst economic downturn since the Great Depression had begun.

The day would come when I'd realize I was lucky. First, though, I'd have to survive several months of unemployment during which I daily wondered who I was. And when I finally did land another job, it was only to face yet another daily challenge: getting to the men's room before throwing up. Most days I'd just make it, depositing the morning's vomit safely into a toilet. Occasionally I'd be slow and have to wipe it off the edge of the bowl. Either way, afterwards I'd slink back onto the narrow ledge I'd grabbed to break my dizzying fall: the hellish newsroom of a small weekly paper called the *Los Angeles Business Journal*.

I understood, of course, that I was fortunate to be employed at all. Being dropped from the *Times*' roster almost in the same month as watching the value of my retirement account drop 30 percent had wreaked havoc on my psyche. So I did what any normal person would: stocked up on Lorazepam to stave off panic attacks, developed an intimate relationship with Ambien to get some sleep and started taking anti-depressants to keep from jumping off a bridge. Then I brushed off my resume and made the rounds.

I was not wildly optimistic regarding the potential results. I had, after all, already reached my 59th year, hardly the vision of a malleable young buck. Newspaper journalism had obviously embarked on its dying throes. And predictions of an economic turnaround were bleak at best. But one day the executive editor of the *Business Journal* called, and a few hours later we were having a chat.

"How would you feel about working with people considerably younger than yourself?" he wanted to know.

"No problem," I replied, and so the deal was sealed.

Though it was gainful employment, the situation was far from ideal. For starters, I had to drive more than an hour each way. Sometimes during rush hour the drive home took as long as two. For the first time in twenty years, I was wearing coats and ties on the job. And for less than half my previous salary, I was doing twice the work. In addition to which, I was covering a subject about which I knew little and cared even less.

In other words, I had fallen into a real job.

I probably could have dealt with all of it. What I couldn't deal with, however, was the re-entry into my life of a species I recognized but thought I'd left far behind: the borderline bipolar newsroom tyrant. Unfortunately, this little paper with big pretensions had more than its share. It didn't help, of course, that most of them were half my age and about that experienced.

I knew I was in trouble the day I saw the managing editor loudly berate a reporter in front of the whole newsroom staff. "What are you, *stupid*?" he asked as she silently stared trembling at the floor. I knew the situation was intolerable, though, when the same thing happened to me. Well, not exactly the same; in my case it was the *executive* editor and the dressing down took place in his office. Actually, the room's glass walls made it more like the control room at San Onofre. And being beckoned into its cushy interior felt precisely like getting a summons from the principal at school.

"So," he said, getting right to the point, "l understand you don't know about AEG."

AEG, I had learned that very morning, stood for Anschutz Entertainment Group, the city's largest provider of live music and purveyor of a popular venue called LA Live. Interviewing the company spokesman for a story, I'd had the temerity to ask exactly what it was that they did.

"The spokesman called me," the editor went on, his voice rising in anger, "and I really didn't know what to say! How can you call yourself a business reporter when you don't even know AEG?"

The answer was, of course, that I couldn't. And so I began planning my escape. The opportunity presented itself a short time later in a most surprising way; an announcement by my wife that she was pregnant. The situation was unusual at best; I was 61, she 29, and we were starting a new family. Friends looked at me like I was crazy, and often I thought they were right.

Gradually, though, I began to see some opportunities in what others were calling a calamity. Beyond the simple joy of having a new child in my life to adore, the most obvious one was this: Ivy, who had a degree in medical technology and was studying for a license to work as a clinical laboratory scientist, was at the beginning of a career that she loved. I, on the other end, was nearing the end of one I'd come to hate. It seemed like the perfect time to switch roles.

On November 28, 2010, our son Isaac came screeching into the world. It was by no means an easy entry; after 24 hours of hard labor, the doctors had finally taken pity on my poor wife and performed a Caesarian section. But even that wasn't easy; she ended up having to stay in the hospital for a blood transfusion, while Isaac was sent to the neonatal intensive care unit for treatment that lasted a week.

The first time we visited him there was hard to forget: of the twelve babies on the ward, only one was screaming. "That one's yours," a nurse informed us, a little too cheerfully I thought. "He's mad because he's hungry; he always wants more than we can give."

That pretty much set the tone for the next several years, which began six weeks later when Ivy returned to her job at the laboratory, and I applied for family leave from mine at the newspaper. "What you're telling me is that I'm going to lose a reporter for two months?" the editor exclaimed in obvious disbelief and displeasure. "No one's ever done that to me before."

"Well I'm sorry to be the first, sir, but it's a benefit to which I'm entitled."

What I knew that he didn't, of course, was that I would never be back. Exiting the newsroom for the last time, I took a long lingering look at the environment in which I'd spent most of my adult life. For years I had aspired to this and now could hardly wait to leave. Finally I took a deep breath and sauntered into the night.

Thus my life entered a new phase dominated by a different kind of deadline.

David Haldane

33.

Green Leafy Space

We're sitting at fast-food restaurant Jollibee in Surigao City in the Philippines, when my cell phone rings with devastating news. It's our new lawyer, who minces no words. "Mr. Haldane," he says. "I'm sorry to tell you that you can't buy the lot." The problem for him is that we've already been warned.

The alarm was tripped by an earlier call from Ivy's old school chum, who hails from Punta Bilar and helped us find that lot in the first place. "Does this guy really represent you?" she had asked, "because he's here right now trying to buy it for *himself*."

The lawyer's call came exactly 15 minutes later. "The seller has too many children who could challenge the sale," he said, "I can't recommend that you consummate the deal."

Biting my lip, I tried to control my rising anger. "We discussed this yesterday," I said as evenly as I could. "You concluded that it was a calculated risk well worth taking."

"I've changed my mind," he said, and that's when my earlier glimpse of the man behind the curtain propelled me into a virtual collision with the ceiling.

"We've already agreed to close the deal," I snapped, "what part of that did you not understand?"

In fairness, there was some merit to the lawyer's alleged concerns. Land transactions in the Philippines, I'd learned from bitter experience, can sometimes be hinky. For starters, as a foreigner I could not own land directly; it would have to be in Ivy's name.

Far more troubling, though, was that this particular parcel was untitled. In other words, it had been in the same family for decades – perhaps even centuries – handed down through generations without the benefit of formal legal recognition. Basically there would be two documents available to us as proof of ownership: a notarized deed of sale showing what we had paid for the property, and a city tax declaration indicating that we were subsequently responsible for all its financial liabilities. Neither would completely shield us from challenge. A legal process pursued later, however, could ultimately generate a title which *would* constitute an almost foolproof shield.

We had discussed all this with the lawyer, who happened to be the brother of a friend. He had listened, considered it carefully or so he claimed, and then advised us to proceed. Now he'd thought better of it, apparently driven by a more personal agenda. Suddenly we felt some urgency about closing the deal.

That happened the next morning at the offices of *another* prominent local attorney, this time fairly perfunctorily. The meeting seemed almost like a Las Vegas wedding; he briefly explained the process – to which we all nodded our ascent – and then Ivy and the seller, a patronly gentleman named Francisco Santillana, stood up and affixed their signatures to the papers that would make it legal. Fifteen minutes later the whole group – sans lawyer but including me, Ivy's parents, several siblings and Francisco's wife with a handful of grown children – were gathered at the bank.

The agreed-upon price was 1.5 million pesos, then about $33,000 U.S. dollars. "How do you want to be paid?" I asked with Ivy's help in translating. "I can do a direct transfer or write you a check."

"Cash only," Santillana insisted, bearing a toothy grin surrounded by sagging cheeks.

And so, as we all sat and watched, a bank teller opened the heavy door and entered the vault. A fair amount of time passed. Finally she emerged carrying a stack of peso notes up to her chin and, carefully counting out the money, deposited it into a large shopping bag brought by Santillana for the purpose. When it was done, the old man grinned widely and then, accompanied by his wife and offspring, promptly exited to the street and disappeared with bag in tow.

I could actually feel my heart rate returning to normal.

A few hours later, Ivy and I were back at our lovely lot by the sea. To get to the top of the hill on which it lay, we had to navigate through tall grass, literally pushing our way forward across uneven ground. It seemed to take a long time and when we finally reached the top we were both out of breath. But when we turned around to catch the view, the oxygen refilled our lungs and reanimated our souls.

Stretching beneath us to our left, a thick grove of coconut trees shimmered verdantly in the sun. Off to the right we could see the coastline arching gracefully south, dotted by fishing villages like ornaments on a string. And directly in front of us, breathtaking in its vastness, the ocean rolled serenely into the mists of the distant islands, shrouding a passing ferryboat emitting wispy gusts of steam. Finally, in the corner of this picture watching like a proud but wary parent, the white Punta Bilar lighthouse stood guarding the scene.

. . .

There are moments in life when everything falls into place, like the pieces of a puzzle finally fitting together to reveal the image they form. Or a bank of clouds suddenly parting to offer a glimpse of the city it had masked. This was just such a moment. For as I took in the wondrous view, it seemed to be completely balanced in a harmony I had never known. And it seemed that I too was part of the picture; that I, like the lighthouse, belonged exactly where I stood. There is no other way of putting this; it felt as if a voice were telling me to stay. This is your place, it seemed to be saying, you have finally come home.

Not too long ago I read a *Wall Street Journal* article entitled "Science Increasingly Makes the Case for God," by Eric Metaxas. Its premise: that the evolution of life on earth is so statistically unlikely, so astronomically incidental given the almost infinite number of environmental factors that had to be aligned, the most accurate way of describing it is as a miracle. In other words, of the various theories explaining how we got here, the one most statistically likely is that we resulted from the intervention of an intelligent Creator.

I don't know whether that is true. Standing on the hill that day, I certainly felt that it was. The only thing remaining was to build our house on this stunning land of God.

David Haldane

Epilogue:

Holding Down the Fort

I'm sitting in the food court at Southern California's Cerritos Mall when I realize that he's gone. It's every parent's nightmare: your 4-year-old son is there and then, well, suddenly he's not. Oh my Lord, I think, please don't let this happen. I hold my breath as everything around me seems to decelerate, distancing itself into a monotonous hum while sliding sideways in slow motion. Then the crowd parts and, like a little Moses traversing the Red Sea, out walks Isaac. "Jesus," I gasp, pulling him hard to my chest, "don't ever do that again."

We'd come to the mall because it was something to do while mommy was at work. He'd been at the slide in the indoor playground while I ate lunch at the food court nearby when all of a sudden I spaced out and looked away for, gosh, a second at most. Oh my, I thought, better not share this with Ivy.

It's the kind of thought not uncommon for stay-at-home dads. Other thoughts include *I've got to be crazy; This is the hardest thing I've ever done; She doesn't really appreciate me;* And *geese, what the hell made me think I could do this?* To which I add one more: *Thank God for this momentous, humbling and glorious time.*

• • •

Taking care of Isaac isn't the only thing I do these days; I also take out the trash, cook frozen dinners and get into pointless – though often highly animated – arguments on Facebook about Israel, the Middle East, domestic politics or whatever else strikes my fancy. Oh, and another thing: I do whatever I can to prepare for our move to the Philippines. To that end, we have completed a design for our dream house; a beautiful four-level Cape Cod-style dwelling with four bedrooms plus a maid's quarters, picture windows, a spiral staircase leading to an observation tower and wraparound patios throughout. The main thing is that it will be built for the view, a house designed so that from every room we can see our lighthouse and the ocean beyond.

I carry a copy of the architect's rendering on my cell phone as sustenance for days when either the weather – or my mood – turns dark. And we have enlisted the aid of a trusted acquaintance to help us traverse the long road to legal entitlement.

In the meantime, our lives are fairly placid. Last week Isaac took a nose dive off the kitchen counter, prompting a trip to the emergency room to ascertain whether any bones had been broken. Fortunately they hadn't; he later explained that he was just being Spiderman. My son's other favorite superheroes include Superman and the Hulk, which has resulted in every breakable object in our house being broken. And when he tires of crashing into Oriental lamps and crystal wine glasses, he enjoys literally bouncing off the walls. Thankfully, our neighbors have gotten somewhat used to the earthquake-like tremors. At least that's what I surmise as neither the police nor department of public social services has been here in more than a month.

• • •

Occasionally, strangers still call me grandpa. It used to annoy me no end, but eventually I made peace with the reality that it reflects. These days when somebody at Walmart or Target assumes I'm Isaac's grandfather, I just smile and say, "Believe it or not, I'm actually his *dad.*" I must admit that I enjoy their initial shock, which sometimes even turns to admiration.

We still hang out with our mixed-couple friends, and I am happy to say that I have made peace with all of my wives. In fact, they have made peace with each other; there are days when my first wife – who is Isaac's Godmother – drops him off at the second wife's house where he is later picked up by the third wife, Isaac's mom. All of this, I believe, is as it should be; I am grateful that the silt has finally settled in my cave, thus clearing a path to the future.

Three days a week, I take my son to preschool along with pumpkins, dried leaves, family photos and whatever else his class happens to be discussing at the time. And those are the days I reflect on how far I've come and how far I yet have to go.

People ask how I will spend my time living on a hill next to a lighthouse overlooking the ocean, and the truth is that I'm not sure. I imagine spending a certain amount of time resting in hammocks. There are still a few native drinks I haven't tried. I will probably do a little scuba diving and lots of walking. And, of course, I will be entertaining friends and relatives with pig-on-a-spit.

Beyond that I have no idea, and that's exactly how I like it. For as I review the chapters of my life, I see that, as unconnected as they seemed at the time, in retrospect they make a book. And so, God willing, I will start a new chapter soon.

There are dark days when the sun isn't shining either in the sky or in my soul, when the road seems too long and the hammock way too far. On days like that I think of home, my green leafy space, my Punta Bilar.

Acknowledgements

There are many who contributed to the development of this work. First and foremost, I wish to thank Ron Featheringill, a lifelong friend who has always had my back and who first suggested this book. Without him, it might never have been written. It was Martin J. Smith, the editor-in-chief of Orange Coast magazine, who first encouraged me to write about how I met and courted my wife, something that might not otherwise have ever been recorded. And the suggestions of Marc Ballon, my friend and editor, were invaluable. Along the way there were many other friends, editors and colleagues who provided important opportunities at critical points in my life and career. Some are mentioned in this book; the others know who they are. To all of them I am eternally grateful. Finally, I wish to thank the members of various writing groups, most notably Coffee House Writers of Long Beach, who read early versions of these chapters, provided valuable input and, most importantly, gave me the confidence to believe that someone somewhere might find them interesting to read.

Purchase other Black Rose Writing titles at www.blackrosewriting.com/books and use promo code PRINT to receive a 20% discount.

www.ingramcontent.com/pod-product-compliance
Lightning Source LLC
Chambersburg PA
CBHW052030070526
44584CB00016B/1981